JESUS
IN
JEANS

JESUS
IN
JEANS

MARY JO ARMEN

TATE PUBLISHING
AND ENTERPRISES, LLC

Published by Tate Publishing & Enterprises, LLC
127 E. Trade Center Terrace | Mustang, Oklahoma 73064 USA
1.888.361.9473 | www.tatepublishing.com

Tate Publishing is committed to excellence in the publishing industry. The company reflects the philosophy established by the founders, based on Psalm 68:11,
"The Lord gave the word and great was the company of those who published it."

Published in the United States of America

ISBN: 978-1-62510-106-8
1. Self-Help / General
2. Self-Help / Spiritual
13.10.07

DEDICATION

This book is dedicated to my husband, who jumped on the peace train without hesitation and met each step of this journey with unconditional love.

My children ChristyAnn, Mia, and Devin, who were excited to call me a writer.

My mom, who has led by example my entire life. My dad, who although was only physically with me for the first eight years of my life, his eternal presence remains with me always. And my stepdad, who has taught me the meaning of true love.

My sisters, who understand my journey and never for a moment doubted this calling, along with my two brothers, who departed this world prematurely, but their presence remains with me always. And my earthly brother who taught me the meaning of unconditional love and forgiveness.

Very special friends, like sisters, who never doubted me and are the managers of my every thought throughout this calling.

Every priest on this path who has taught me with each and every homily they delivered. They left me hungry and thirsty, craving for more.

Finally, I want to acknowledge my two sisters, the true editors, who ran along side of me to bring the completion of this book to the finish line.

CONTENTS

INTRODUCTION

I am an everyday jeans and t-shirt kind of girl, a girl who grew up in a home that oozed Catholicism, a girl who attended Catholic school from kindergarten to college. A daily dose of faith was as routine as breathing. Throughout my life, I have always felt the presence of God. I have always walked around with a sense of peace. However, I never really stopped to think about it. I assumed everyone was aware of God's presence in his life and everyone felt the peace that I felt.

Recently, this constant peace in my life grew exponentially when I was attending the closing Mass for a pre-Cana weekend. I was serving as a member of the team. During Mass, a peace so great surrounded me that I truly felt as if I was floating. I looked around to notice if everyone was "floating" in this peace bubble. I even asked my husband if he was feeling what I was feeling. To my dismay, I was the only one in this peace bubble. As the days went on, this feeling of peace grew stronger and stronger and stronger. I felt as if I had to do something with it. I thought of people who I could reach out to, in hopes of offering them the peace I was feeling.

This peace led me to writing spiritual essays to my friend, whom I refer to as the editor. She is a friend who, over the years, has proofread professional reports written for work. It seemed very natural to share my thoughts with her via email. The thoughts wouldn't stop coming. My "editor" became the manager of my spiritual thoughts. I noted every thought, prayer, and moment of feeling God's presence.

I was drawn to my computer every day. I was drawn to attend Mass every day. My writing eventually changed from emails to the chapters that you are about to read. I have faith that as you enter my peace bubble, you will never want to leave it. I encourage you to read this book as you would sip and savor your favorite beverage. I suggest getting cozy. It is my hope that in reading these divinely inspired words, your heart will change throughout each and every chapter as mine did.

Cheers to sharing in my journey! Cheers to opening your heart! Cheers to embracing your journey!

May God bless you as you enjoy every sip.

THE BEGINNING

From: Mary Jo Armen
Subject: Thank You
Date: April 3, 2011 7:30 p.m.

Dear Penny,

It is with humility, grace, and gratitude that I send this email.

Several years ago when we were asked to become a part of the pre-Cana team[1], I thought it was very simple. Volunteer my time for a weekend, and be my loving and welcoming self to newly engaged couples. I thought it was a one-shot deal to be checked off the list until I found a ministry that would work for my family. But pre-Cana was a big-time commitment that involved babysitters, arranging of schedules, etc. I became a Eucharistic minister[2] and words can't express how awestruck I am each and every time I serve at a Mass. It was simple. I had my ministry.

This year when I saw the email, I thought, "Good Lord, my resignation letter of last year did not take!" Kicking and screaming, I agreed to serve on pre-Cana. But this time it was different. I felt called...called in a way that is hard to put into words. Serving today, is God's gift to Chris and me, and for that, I am so thankful. I had that "Cornerstone[3] feeling." I think you know what I am talking about. I even called my mom from the car to have a quick discussion on the gifts of the Holy Spirit and God's grace. We chatted briefly. I entered for pizza. I have, and continue to have, this presence around me... not sure what I am supposed to do with it, but I will figure it out. Becoming more of a "giving" member on the team is a start. I will be patient and continue to listen to God's call, which right now is so very overwhelming. I have been humbled by today's experience.

God clearly has given me the grace to have the courage to email you these thoughts.

In closing, I would like to thank you from the bottom of my heart, for allowing us to serve.

With much gratitude,
Mary Jo and Chris

(Just as I was about to hit send, Chris looked over my shoulder and said, "You're not putting my name?" Clearly we are one!)

From: Mary Jo Armen
Date: Mon, 11 Apr 2011 2:00 p.m.
To: Patty
Subject: Spiritual ADD *(Attention Deficit Disorder)* getting worse...

I cannot focus on anything other than this. What is this? A calling? I don't even know how to label it. My work schedule is not confirmed for the week, my bank deposit isn't getting done, and I have no desire to return calls for tutoring appointments. This really isn't me. I cannot afford to be distracted like this. But all I want to do is search, and read, and be in church, as a source of comfort until I can figure this out.

There is a part of me that is starting to go out of my mind. What can I do to alleviate this? If there was Mass right at this moment I'd be there.

Am I explaining myself clearly? I really am trying so hard to manage it.

I am not fighting it like I have done in the past. Will it pass after Lent? Is this a Lenten sacrifice? Could this just be an exercise on testing my mental strength? (which is quite strong but I always worry because of my brother Paul's struggles... not to worry, I am not cracking... just stating a fact that remains a mystery to me.) I have to get my head in the game of life.

From: Patty
Subject: RE: Spiritual ADD (*Attention Deficit Disorder*) getting worse...
Date: April 11, 2011 2:39 p.m.
To: Mary Jo

I cannot explain why all these thoughts keep swirling around. *Breathe, relax, breathe.*

Hopefully reading the book to Devin will help. Too bad there isn't an off switch so you could go back to all the daily tasks of your life. Have you ever read the book *Eat, Pray, Love?*

From: Mary Jo Armen
Sent: Thursday, April 14, 2011 1:14 p.m.
To: Patty
Subject: the journey has started

Another day, another run...

As every day should start, this morning I went to Mass, and what I realized is that today, April 14, will be a special day for me because I am starting on the next part of my journey with an earthly angel. An angel I am so very blessed to have. I have had many angels in my life but they are heavenly.

To have one at your own disposal who can deliver peace in a moment, wisdom unknowingly, humility at every moment, and grace on a platter, is a blessing that is too overwhelming to comprehend. It could leave some of us speechless.

On this very special day, as I enjoyed the beauty of the sun shining, I went for a run with a friend, who has been an angel for me during a time, when my heart ached from life's hurts. And with God's grace, she appeared at the exact moment that I needed her to carry me. She was Jesus to me. Today, as I am ready to forgive all the hurts and move on, here she appears at my side. God is with me.

We run without a route or amount of miles in mind. For she shares my same running philosophy: it's about fellowship and friendship. We spoke of mutual friends who were experiencing troubles in their lives. We spoke of faith and having God's presence in your life. We discussed how life is not a perfect place and it's what you choose to make of it. We are all in control of our reality. As we caught up and listened to each other's stories, we ended with a list of friends for whom we needed to pray. We mentioned each by name. Some I know and some names I am hearing for the first time. Isn't that what we are called to do?

The power of prayer still amazes me. The transforming power of prayer is so very powerful. For me, it is putting me on a path that I cannot question, yet I have to pursue. Actually pursuing it is not a choice, for it is a calling that is so very hard to put into words. Questioning it, is like questioning God, and who am I to question Him? So I travel on a path that is unknown. For me it is exciting to see where it will lead. With my silent partner, my personal angel, I have great faith that we will be doing great things. For we have an equation that has been in the making for many years. With the perfect equation, it is very possible to conquer the world.

From: Patty
Subject: RE: the journey has started
Date: April 15, 2011 8:12 a.m.
To: Mary Jo Armen

I am just checking email for the first time in 24 hours. What you say is so beautifully written, but it always is. I think my role is listener and editor. When I talk too much or have too many opinions, I can hear a voice (or have a feeling) that says, "Enough, time to be quiet." And, I heard it yesterday, so now I will be quiet.

I like the way you weave math in at the end. Maybe the title is Math and Faith. Yes, they can coexist. :) I can't run or yoga today. I am going golfing. It is a great day to be outside. Enjoy.

Patty

From: Mary Jo Armen
Subject: An ironic God
Date: April 15, 2011 1:22 p.m.
To: Patty

Dear Editor,

I am in a very tough spot. While I respect the silent editing, I do not understand it. This is my challenge that I will try to understand. While I am trying to understand it, the teacher in me would love for it to be defined. I am not trying to be a jackass. Truly, I respect you way too much. I just do not get it. I am the math student who is trying to understand a concept that needs to be approached verbally and the teacher has handed me visual clues. I am, respectfully, at a loss. I get that my words are torturing you just as your silence is torturing me. Is there a happy medium? I have not chosen what is happening. I would never intentionally put either one of us in this situation. While there are people in my life who are not tortured by my words, they *do not get this*, with the exception of my mother. How can I expect anyone to get this because I don't? I have tried to reach out to Fr. Neutral with no response (which, by the way, was not so easy). So, my thoughts are out there, and not one syllable or guidance about it. Is there a handbook? I will read it. Are things of this nature to be handled in silence? Is that why you are on this road with me? If that is the case and this is the journey, I will accept it.

This situation is now causing Chris to become anxious because it is so totally unknown.

So the person that is the biggest source of the managing of my thoughts on a daily basis is unavailable and I need to be available to him. Again, another challenge: to be supportive to another when you are in your own turmoil, which is spiritual. The irony of this situation is that while I have words for everyone on this planet, not one person has words for me. I do not have the words for myself to make sense of this. So I think, do I call Dr. M and sort out spirituality with a Jewish therapist? The other side is to dismiss it...which I tried to do at yoga today... and here's the story that I wasn't going to write...

While in yoga today, trying to lie to rest the thoughts that I cannot control, I became lightheaded, which happens when you practice yoga in 104 degree heat but usually not to me. I did the responsible thing, and with humility, I got into the child's pose, all while trying to dismiss the thoughts of the spiritual mess that I am in. Within moments, the girl next to me gets into the child's pose and stops her practice. She is a like a pro and I have never ever seen her go down. When the third person gets into the child's pose, the instructor comes to our corner and jokingly says, "I think the *devil* is in this corner, take as much time as you need." With that I am right back on this jackass path praying for God to be at my side. Because to me, the mention of the *devil* is no joke...not for a second.

So here I am in a mess that I cannot escape. Part of me sees it as exciting and is happy to sprint toward it and let it happen, which I am doing as I write. I am experiencing the challenges that Jeremiah faced in this morning's reading (Jer 20:10-13). I have had many other challenges in my life that I have overcome. I too, can overcome this, and find the lesson that I am supposed to learn.

This has been a very difficult day on a road that I did not choose.

With the utmost respect,
Anonymous

From: Mary Jo Armen
Date: Fri, 15 Apr 2011 5:55 p.m.
To: Patty
Subject: Spiritual IEP (Individualized Education Program)[4]

This is a good one!

Background Information: A Catholic girl raised in a home that oozed Catholicism. The youngest of six children. Currently, Mary Jo resides in River Edge with her husband, Chris, and three children. She presents as a peaceful spirit who is finding her way on the Road to Emmaus[5].

Reason for Referral: Mary Jo has been experiencing some overwhelming feelings that she expresses as a calling. It appears that she cannot fully put it into words how this is manifesting. She describes a desire to be in church as often as possible, for this brings her peace. Again she uses the word *calling* to describe this feeling. She is seeing spiritual signs all around her that point toward the Road to Emmaus. She has a desire to write and write and write. Mary Jo finds comfort in being with others who try to understand this calling. At times, she can be troubled by the uncertainty that is ahead. While welcoming the challenge, it is overwhelming and exciting at the same time.

Spiritual IEP:
1) Respect silence
2) Stop trying to figure out the path
3) Express thanks that you are on the road and recognize a companion
4) Roll with it, write at will
5) Have faith in the editor
6) Relax
7) Spread the peace and love in your heart
8) Embrace John's gospel of Jesus' teaching: "If you continue in my word, you are truly my disciples, and you will know the truth, and the truth will set you free."
9) Enjoy the journey
10) Remember my mother's words, "You are not Jesus."
11) Amen

* * *

From: Patty
Subject: re: Spiritual IEP
Date: April 16, 2011 8:05 a.m.
To: Mary Jo

Love it. No editing needed.

From: Mary Jo Armen
Subject: clarification
Date: April 16, 2011 8:11 a.m.
To: Patty

Patty,

Please know that my bombarding you via text the other day with questions, like "is this normal?", "does this happen to others?", etc. was an attempt for me to make sense of what the heck is going on. It is how my brain works when it processes information. I am a logical thinker and I was trying too hard to find a logical explanation for something that I will not have a concrete answer to. This is part of my thinking and thought process. I need to talk when I process things. I have accepted this path and have learned not to question it. For when I did, I had an *awful* day. I am done with the questioning. I expect not one word from you with these questions…not one. I apologize for making you nuts. I get it because I made myself nuts. This is not an easy thing, but I am doing my very best to roll with it. I appreciate your patience, and like I said earlier, I admire your silence. Thanks for not upsetting the balance and having the wisdom to respond in the way that you did.

A million thanks,
Mary Jo

From: Mary Jo Armen
Subject: this gift
Date: April 16, 2011 2:14 p.m.
To: Patty

Am I supposed to do something with this other than what I am doing? Are others aware of my gift? If this is met with silence, I get it and will follow my IEP. I am in awe. Simply stated: thank you.

From: Mary Jo Armen
Subject: sleeping with God
Date: April 17, 2011 10:27 a.m.
To: Patty

So here I am with God's overwhelming presence at all times. He knows my every thought, my every move, my every breath. I feel His every move, His every thought, His every breath. It is like we are one. As I sit to write an essay I thought I wasn't going to write, I wonder where have these words come from. I think we know the answer. Because at this very moment, I am not in control of my destiny. As I embrace this journey, I experience a roller coaster of emotions. It has been a calling that at times leaves those around me speechless. It is not a game. For if it was, I would quit. It is exhausting and all consuming. But how can you quit God? He is here and ever present.

As I share this experience with my husband, there is a transformation that is occurring, for he is an anxious person and I fear that telling him will cause a heightened anxiety. When I can no longer contain what I am feeling, I have no choice but to tell him. I tell him my every thought, my every feeling, my every fear. I am met with compassion, understanding, and nothing but unconditional love. I have always felt my love for Chris to be extraordinary and his for me equal. We are a balanced equation of equal overpowering love, a love as strong as the oneness I feel with God at this moment. Our love, if possible, has gotten stronger. So here I am to say, "Bring it on! Let's get this party started!"

Amen

From: Mary Jo Armen
Subject: a new life…a new day
Date: April 18, 2011 9:36 a.m.
To: Patty

Life has become a different place…the one it was always meant to be. While I try to comprehend the fact that my every thought is shared with God, I find a sense of peace, a peace that reaches the core of my being. A peace that all in this world should know and feel. And as I feel this peace, my day starts with my husband, who momentarily is not at peace, for he awoke from a nightmare, one that evoked anxiety. With an embrace, a silent prayer that I know is being heard, he asks me to pray aloud for his peace. The silence is broken. A transformation is occurring before my eyes. A transformation that gives my husband the desire to attend 8:00 a.m. Mass with me. A transformation that allows me to feel the greatest student-teacher interaction I have ever felt in my entire life… placing communion in the hands of the children from St. Peter's Academy. This excitement was rather ridiculous. I felt stupidly giddy to the point that I tried to contain my smile, but couldn't.

What a beautiful start to this day. How blessed am I?

From: Patty
Subject: re: a new life...a new day
Date: April 18, 2011 9:45 a.m.
To: Mary Jo

Wow...speechless. Your calm presence has caught on. That is wonderful that he experienced this miracle and freedom. Best of all he is looking to you for help, prayers, and healing.

From: Mary Jo Armen
Sent: Monday, April 18, 2011 10:14 a.m.
To: Patty
Subject: a miracle has occurred…(in my eyes)

Read a new life…a new day first. (Heart is in your hands now more so than ever…handle with care.)

In my eyes a miracle has occurred. For the 21 years that I have been with my husband, he has battled anxiety. At times, it was so very bad. The best medicine has been unconditional love. Because I am not perfect there were many moments where I had lost my patience. For me, what always brought me back to the place of unconditional love was my faith. The faith that one day there would be peace. This miracle has been a prayer that has been with me for many years. After a silent prayer, a prayer lacking silence, and morning Mass, it has occurred via text message (for I am the modern-day Jesus in Jeans): "I feel ready to let it all go. Everything. If I need help I want it from you." My hands are shaking as I type. You truly have no idea what this means to me. No idea.

From: Mary Jo Armen
Subject: God is cleaning my house
Date: April 19, 2011 9:15 a.m.
To: Patty

As I awoke this morning and noticed God's silence, I became concerned. Did He leave? Was this just a short visit? For if it was, I would be so sad. With this thought came another, perhaps He is silent. There had been so much dialogue most recently. I had forgotten the sound of silence. With this realization, I put my thoughts to rest. He is with me. Still yearning to hear His voice, for I am known to be a chatty person, I think about going to 8:00 a.m. Mass. Unsure if I want to leave the warmth of my bed, I lie silently as I contemplate. The silence is broken with my husband's voice who says, "I'll meet you at Mass on my way home from the gym. Can I go in gym clothes?" (Fashion first is the motto in this house.) Without hesitation, I agree to the plan. While at Mass, I start my conversation with my friend, God. As you can tell, I have a hard time with silence. Clearly it is a lesson I am trying to master. With a failing grade in the subject of silence, I make a deal with God. I've done this in the past and have never been disappointed.

I ask Him to allow me to be on the altar as a Eucharistic minister and, to up the ante, I make the bold request for the chalice. With the request granted, as I stand on the altar, I offer a prayer for my husband to have everlasting peace. I was a bit disappointed when the priest instructed me to the side opposite of where my husband would receive. I forgot one tiny detail of the request. But as I look up my husband *is* on my communion line. God knows my every thought.

Upon coming home, I greet my cleaning lady, Maria, who has become another member of this family. We talk faith, finances, family – you name it, we discuss it. With Maria there is a presence of love and genuine concern every moment I am in her company. When she asks about Chris, I tell her that he is on his way home because he met me at Mass. To which she says, "Ah Miss Mari (try to hear a Spanish accent), you husband went to pray with you? Do jou (you) remember last time I was here you went to church?" I clearly had forgotten and asked her to remind me. She continues to say that I attended Mass and when she asked me why, my reply was simple, "I am praying for my husband to have a greater faith, for it will bring him peace." With that she says, "Oh, Miss Mari, don't you see, God has answered your prayer."

Who knew God cleans toilets?

From: Mary Jo Armen
Subject: prayer
Date: April 23, 2011 9:20 a.m.
To: Patty

Almighty and Eternal God, You have brought us together through our faith. During this sacred time of the Resurrection of Christ, continue to be with us as we open our hearts, for we are called to be together.

TRIDUUM

As I was being pulled to my computer this morning to write, I sat in front of the screen and nothing...not a thought, not a word, not a finger running across the keys. So I got up, walked away, and tried to tend to my life, confirming appointments for work. But there it was again, the magnetic attraction to the computer. So I sat. As I sat, it came to me: silence. During the Easter celebration, there had been so much energy around me and so much great work being done, that I had forgotten silence. I had almost forgotten the value of silence. For during these moments, we can appreciate the peace that surrounds us. I had begun to look forward to hearing the sound of God's voice. It was like looking forward to a special occasion.

Quite frankly, I was not sure if I would be hearing His voice anytime soon. I thought we both must have had laryngitis. For the talking that had taken place over the Triduum[6] was extraordinary. I had a feeling about what was going to happen. It was more than a feeling. I also had faith that on Easter Sunday this "calling" would have more clarity. So, as not to disappoint me, the vision rolled in as clear as day. While some might have seen it as a joke, I certainly did not. And if anyone cared to see it as a joke, I would have put an end to any such thoughts, for I would not have allowed anyone to make a joke of God's work. Even as I write this, I am still in awe that an Aisle 7 ShopRite spiritual girl was in this situation. Growing up in my very religious family, I was the least likely person I would have thought that God would call. My siblings seemed way more faith-filled and religious than me. But perhaps it was hard for me to see it in myself. It's like a tree trying to recognize it's part of a forest. It would have been much easier if God had sent me a text, because His communication, while it was full of fast-paced energy, was also exhausting. His gift to me was that it happened while I had a week off from work.

I will make an attempt to explain the lightning-speed communication, but I am not sure that I can do it justice. Thank God my "editor" was at my side, for she was a witness to an energy that took over my very being, an energy that could have stopped a train in motion, truly an unbelievable energy. The results of this energy were "mini" miracles (in my eyes) happening all around me. Ready, set, go!

Holy Thursday started with a midday prayer gathering for priests. As I was so excited to go to this, I was also aware of the transformation that was happening in my life. Why was I at church and not shopping for the perfect Easter outfit? While I didn't find the perfect outfit in church, I found more peace, if that was possible. The peace bubble got so big that I felt as if I was floating on this cloud of peace without my feet touching the ground. Floating home, I started to look forward to evening Mass of the Lord's Supper. Again, why wasn't I thinking of an evening out with a glass of wine? In accordance with my Spiritual IEP, I rolled with it! As excited as I was to attend Mass, I was also disappointed that I would not have the opportunity to be on the altar as a Eucharistic minister. While I sat in Mass, I was beaming with excitement and a sense of pride, all while loving that my family was with me. Without expecting to be on the altar, I landed there anyway, for an earthly angel, in the form of a friend, approached and gently suggested leaving the balcony to get our feet washed. This was a selfless act. Knowing my friend the way I do, I am sure that she was not interested in being front and center. With uncontainable excitement, I enthusiastically took off both shoes to hear the priest chuckle and say, "Just one," ever so softly. I think I would have jumped in for an entire bath and baptism if he had let me! It seemed appropriate to be baptized for my soul felt reborn.

With the close of Mass, there was a procession of the Blessed Sacrament[7] that ended in the chapel for adoration during night prayer. I gathered my family and we sat in the Lord's presence. Powerful.

Upon going home, I anticipated going back to the chapel to pray. This didn't surprise me because even with my Aisle 7 ShopRite spirituality, I always enjoyed the solitude and peace of praying in the presence of the Blessed Sacrament. What made this visit so special was that I had asked my sister, who has always been a Jesus freak, to join me. Unbeknownst to me, there was a tradition of "church hopping" that took place on Holy Thursday. You were to visit as many churches as you could to represent staying with Jesus. Naturally, my sister was church hopping when I called with my request for her to meet me at the chapel. The irony of this, was that suddenly, my so-not-Jesus-freak self, became a bit jealous of her church hopping, which I would have giggled about not too long ago. I was beginning to realize that I might have to attend a Jesus freak anonymous support group: "Hello, my name is Mary Jo and I am a Jesus-loving freak. I have become obsessed with teaching His way. It is my goal to teach anyone who will listen." With this realization, I took my Jesus freak self to the chapel to pray.

Walking into the chapel was magical. I was overcome with an energy, an energy so powerful that I was unaware of anyone around me. Bruce Springsteen could have been sitting behind me and I wouldn't have known. But if I had become aware of his presence, I would have definitely convinced him to write a ballad about my Jesus freak journey. He would absolutely have agreed. Unfortunately, for both him and me, he was not in attendance; however, my sister was. She came in, sat next to me, and handed me a daily prayer book called *The Magnificat.*[8] Who knew what this book was and why one would even have it? She opened it to a reading about a temptation of Jesus. I was so much in the zone that I had to read it twice in order to have full comprehension. Clearly, I didn't retain the information because, as I am now writing, I am unable to even summarize this temptation. As I said, I was in a zone. Perhaps you can understand what I read:

Adoration Vigil for Holy Thursday Night
by Monsignor Lorenzo Albacete

...Second Vigil

If you are the Son of God, throw yourself down. For it is written,/ "He will command his angels concerning you,"/ and, "with their hands they will support you,/ lest you dash your foot against a stone." Mt 4:6

Put your sword back into its sheath, for all who take the sword will perish by the sword. Do you think that I cannot call upon my Father and he will not provide me at this moment with more than twelve legions of angels?

Mt 26:52-53

Meditation

Once again the Tempter strikes at the relation between Jesus and the Father. "If you are the Son of God..." Jesus is tempted to question the mystery of his own identity. All temptations aim at denying the truth of the mystery of the Incarnation. St. John the Evangelist writes that the Holy Spirit, the "Spirit of Truth," can be recognized because he does not separate the Son of God from the flesh, that is, because he confirms the identity of Jesus as the Incarnate Son of the Father. The spirit that separates the Son of God from the flesh is the Anti-Christ, the spirit of the "lie" (cf. 1Jn. 4, 1-3).

In this temptation, the Tempter argues that if Jesus is the Son of God, he would be able to avoid his death. We experience this temptation when we wonder why the followers of Jesus are not spared death. It is our fear of death that gives temptation its power. But Jesus did not avoid his confrontation with death. He exposes himself to the fear of death in order to conquer it with the confidence that comes from the love that unites him with the Father. He will defeat death by freely embracing his death with absolute confidence. God is love, and love is stronger than death.

Jesus himself pointed to the Eucharist as the means to overcome the power of death. His Body and Blood are the source of a life that is stronger than the power of death, a life sustained by the power of the Love that is God. Jesus remains with us in the Blessed Sacrament precisely as the proclamation of the victory of God's love over death. The Eucharist is his reply to the temptation, emptying it of its power. Allowing the Eucharist to shape our life will free us too from the fear of death.

Lord Jesus Christ present in the Eucharist as the Son of God in human flesh. Your presence is the source of a life stronger than death. Strengthen our frail humanity by the power of the Holy Spirit, that we might be powerful witnesses that death is not the last word about human destiny. Amen....

Acknowledgment: Text excerpted from the Adoration Vigil for Holy Thursday Night by Monsignor Lorenzo Albacete in © MAGNIFCAT

Holy Week edition, 2011, (www.magnificat.
com). Used with permission.

As I started to have greater understanding of what
Jesus endured, I felt as if I was becoming the presi-
dent of the Jesus Lovers Society. A small prayer service began with the close of silent prayer, and then I
returned home to text my "editor", who introduced
a new word: *mystery*. With my new crazed energy, at
that very moment I was not truly enjoying this word.
Mystery, come on, are you kidding me? I wanted a big
fat answer for what was going on in my life and I was
met with *mystery*? Give it up, sister. I would have fired
my editor at that moment, but it is very hard to fire
someone from a job that is part of a calling from God,
for it was a job that had no pay, hence no possibility for
termination. My brilliant editor (I say with *profound*
truth and sarcasm at the same time) followed up her
annoying word with, "There is no answer. It is just a
mystery." Not wanting to accept this, I must ask if mys-
teries have answers. Her response via text: "Never. We
believe something we can't see, touch, taste, smell…
mystery." With my need to have an answer, I struggled
with this response. I was then advised to give it to God.

What came with my interpretation of mystery was
that I might deny this calling, in turn deny God, because
I was being tempted to give it up with the mention of
the word *mystery*. I did not understand that what was
happening was a mystery, which was the calling. While
there was no explanation for the calling, there could be
a vision for what the calling would be. I battled these
thoughts as I went to sleep.

This confusion about mystery, and a calling, plagued me the next day, which was Good Friday. Truly I was tortured with my thoughts. I wrote an essay and researched the Paschal Mystery,[9] and found myself on Jesus freak websites that I didn't even know existed, all for the love of God! I had been so narrow-minded, seeing my viewpoint only; nevertheless, I was not willing to give up this calling because I had an undying faith in God, His plan, and the journey. What I didn't realize was that this was part of the journey. My thoughts tortured me so much that I turned them into words via emails to my editor. Now we were both tortured. Why not? After all, it was Good Friday, a day of suffering.

With an attempt to put the thoughts to rest, I went to church to be a part of the Passion of our Lord Jesus Christ. What a beautiful experience being with my entire family including my mom, stepdad, and Jesus-loving sister. It was after the service that the energy grew to a level of absolute crazy intensity, an energy as strong as God's love for us.

Here we go…

I found myself having a conversation with a close family member, who had been estranged for almost 15 years, and encouraged him to come for Easter dinner, an event I thought would never happen. The conversation was as normal as if we had chatted yesterday.

I found out from my sister that a huge prayer of hers had been answered.

My church prayer group that had grown apart was starting to join together through an email invitation. By the end of the day, *all* had been contacted, and most had responded positively, to an invitation to pray at my home.

After a tearful conversation with my husband, my vision started to shape up. Perhaps my call was to create a three-tier level of educating parents, teens, and children about living a simplistic life filled with helping others in their daily routine.

Then, I was prompted to write a talk to give to my church group. Within moments, an essay was written.

At that moment, a feeling of peace engulfed my house, which created a silent hum. My children were at peace playing together and enjoying each other's company. If I had asked them to fight like cats and dogs, I don't even think they would have done so.

I turned the radio on and a song that clearly reminded me of my brother (who is a heavenly angel) was playing. Are you getting the picture?

With all of this swirling around me, I left my house that evening to attend the youth group's Good Friday Passion play with my entire family – very special. As I was sitting in my pew, feeling my phone vibrate, a text came in. My first thought was perhaps it was God, for I am in His house. Time revealed that God did indeed send a text via my editor. It stated,

> Almighty and eternal God, you have restored us to life by the triumphant death and resurrection of Christ. Continue this healing work within us. May we who participate in this *mystery* never cease to serve You. We ask this in the name of Jesus the Lord.

To which I replied, "Amen."

At the end of this day of unrelenting thoughts and being tempted to end my journey, clarification humbled me. My mind was at rest knowing that I would never be like Peter and deny Jesus.

Next stop: Holy Saturday.

The day was filled with peace, bumping into some church group girls unexpectedly, who responded on the spot, to the prayer invitation. While running around, I encountered a friend who was having a bad day, in aisle twelve of Target. We embraced and I listened to her life's hurts. The day ended at Barnes & Noble with my family. I promised the kids all week that they could get books with gift cards I had been given. It was very interesting that this shopping trip hadn't happened all week, but I came to realize that it was intended to happen on Holy Saturday.

While the kids were in the children's section, I started researching existing book titles which I sent to my editor: *My Life with the Saints, Have a New Husband by Friday: How to Change his Attitude, Behavior, Communication, Fearless, Ruthless Trust, The Ragamuffins Path to God, Show us How True Radical Trust in God Can Transform our Lives, Bringing Out the Best in People, How to Enjoy Helping Others Excel, Hearing from God Each Morning: 365 Daily Devotionals, The Power of Prayer to Change your Marriage, Pray FIT.*

After a fun family dinner, it was time to get in bed with hopeful anticipation of Easter Sunday. During the night I woke a little bit after 3:00 a.m. This had become a ritual since the "calling" rolled into town. I had learned that this sudden awakening from sleep was associated with the Divine Mercy Hour, the hour when Jesus died. It happens often to those being called to serve. So, there you have it, God made house calls! Once I noted the thought that awakened me, I could fall immediately back to sleep. I had to learn not to fight it so I could get back to sleep. I noted my thought: pray for a friend. Prayer complete and back to sleep.

With the arrival of Easter morning, I had a childlike excitement. I was ready to wear my new Easter dress that could have been a baptismal gown. It was a white lace overlay on a nude color tank dress. It was simple, yet elegant – perfect for the occasion. As I stepped into the shower, my "phone booth to God," thoughts started rushing into my head like I was watching a movie in fast-forward. I was processing the events of the past three days at lightning speed. An image was forming – an educational building, like on a college campus. Next, the following words came to my mind: spiritual wellness center. I was in awe. It all pulled together. It was no longer a mystery.

I quickly researched the book titles I had stumbled upon the night before in Barnes & Noble. They all fell into this category. It was a family-based spiritual wellness center. How cool is that? When I thought back, I remembered thinking how I would love to work on a college campus; I love the energy of being in a classroom. I would love to teach a course like "How to Lead a Simple Life Containing Daily Acts of Kindness." In addition, I would love to train people for running marathons while discussing God's grace in our lives.

Without being able to contain what I had figured out, I was longing for a conversation. Simultaneously, I texted my editor and told my husband about it. He was down with it. My brother-in-law, Joe, called, and he admitted to having had a vision of me being a spiritual counselor, but had kept it to himself. My Jesus freak sister confirmed the same vision, and that she had read two of the books I had researched. My sister-in-law, Allie, had read another, and my mom yet *another*! Amen. Case closed.

In conclusion, I love being a Jesus *freak*. Who is cooler than me?

Now what?

THE JOURNEY

As I waited for the express bus of words to roll into town, I wondered when the next scheduled stop would be. For you see, there was no rhyme or reason, no schedule that I could have followed. I just waited, and for me, the bus was very reliable. I was learning to depend on it, because without it, there were no words.

With the start of my day, I sensed the silence and the peace that was coupled with it. I was thankful, yet not, for I had grown accustomed to the energy, but it felt like something was missing. When the words took flight, an energy preceded them. It's a wild crazy energy that is like the wind blowing in on a beautiful spring day. And today, while at Dunkin' Donuts, unshowered, with hair that was not my fashion-first best, I knew I needed to buckle up for the ride. Upon going home, I was drawn to the computer. I was not sure why, so I sat. As I sat, it hit me: I was to write to my friend, the editor, about a situation that had been tugging at my heart. It was like I chugged truth serum and I had to release my thoughts. Because I am obedient, I sat, I typed, and when done, I felt cleansed as if I had just left the confessional. My penance followed in the form of a three-mile run.

Before I speak of the run, you must understand that at this time, I was in the final week of training for a half-marathon. My training had been challenging, but I had persevered. I had accepted that this race was going to be slow and steady and realized that I had very much enjoyed the journey. This journey had been one filled with runs, where I had an incredible opportunity to train my dear friend Mary's seventeen-year-old daughter, Caroline, for her first half-marathon. While she was Forrest Gump and I was Mrs. Doubtfire, the pace and age did not matter. For each run had been so special, and had a spirituality within it, as special as God's love for us.

Now yesterday was supposed to be just a short run, because that is what you do the week of the race. In a runner's world, it is called "taper" week. Because you had done your hard work of long runs, you have earned a light week of running before the big day. With that in mind, I set out for an easy run. Expecting it to be a breeze, I was caught off guard when I did not have my wind and my calves were cramping up. I was so very disappointed. This was not the type of run you want to have five days before running a half-marathon. It kills your mental strength and 80 percent of running is mental, but I persevered.

As I was getting discouraged, I saw a priest from my parish pass by and we greeted each other with a big wave. I had the need to keep stopping to catch my breath.

Finally, when I was in front of my church and my legs were so tight, I stood beside the statue of Mother Mary. Then, on three occasions, I tried to take a step and faltered. The third time I had to give up, sat down on the sidewalk, and rubbed my calf. While I was fighting back the tears and disappointment, I was a bit annoyed with my friend, God, who had brought me such peace, and had assisted me to bring it to others. I let Him know that I was less than happy that there was no peace in my running that day, and I found it so very unfair. As I chewed Him out, I was also aware that in darkness there is light, and deep in the core of my soul, I would be thankful for this moment, for good was to come of it. However, while I was in it, because I am human, I was annoyed and let Him know. Eventually, I accepted that this was a junky run, and I walked a little. During the acceptance of this *junky* run, I had no choice but to turn to God and pray knowing that my momentary anger would be forgiven. As a Jesus freak, I embraced my very human actions knowing that through Jesus' life they were understood by God. After all, isn't that why Jesus walked this earth – so that His Divine Being could understand the human nature of this world?

The following day, when I set out for a run, I felt a magical energy around me. Within the first two steps, I thought, "I got this one." While getting into a groove, I saw a gray-haired man running slowly. As I approached he said, "You wouldn't dare pass an old man like me." With that I slowed down and we ran side by side. Because I have not mastered the gift of silence, I started engaging in a conversation about running. He explained that today's run was a recovery run for him because he had injured his back this winter shoveling snow. I shared that I had had a terrible run just yesterday and it had rattled my confidence for the half-marathon on Sunday. He spoke of running five marathons and several half-marathons. Within moments, we bonded and we ran step for step alongside each other. I told him he was my "running angel" for the day because he was exactly what I needed: someone to run with and get my head back in the game. He jokingly said, "I have never been anyone's angel." He then turned to me and said, "I think you are mine. I never have anyone to run with. This is so nice." As we continued to talk, I discovered that I knew his daughter. I remembered that he had lost his wife when his daughter was young. I tried to make a connection for him when he asked my maiden name. I explained that I was a bit older than his daughter, but knew her through a mutual friend. When I mentioned my friend Amy, he hesitated and looked at me, remembering that her brother Todd had died September 11, 2001, in the World Trade Center. He had fond memories of him because he had coached him. I explained that Todd was like a brother to me and that I had lost two of my own brothers, Chris and Paul. He looked me square in the eye and said, "That's nothing you get over." We chatted about how it was something you live with and I acknowledged the loss of his wife. We talked about faith and how we both belonged to the same parish, St. Peter's.

My buddy left me and I continued running. My pace was steady and consistent. I picked it up and headed to the town library. As I approached, I slowed down and entered the September 11 Memorial Garden adjacent to the library. I walked to Todd's memorial stone and prayed in front of it. I gave thanks for he was with me on this run. I made a pebble cross, like I always did, but I noticed something different. His parents always write the word *love* in pebbles, and I saw that, but above their word was something. I looked closely and the word *hope* was scratched into the stone. Noticing that, I etched *peace* and slowly started to run. I felt as if I were running on air and then it occurred to me – peace had come to my running. I continued running and the words "charity begins in the home" came to me. I wondered why. In an instant I realized that those words will be the name of a spiritual wellness center. How cool is that?

Remembering a gospel reading indicating that the "truth shall set you free," I thought of the truth serum email I had sent to my friend, the editor, in conjunction with the darkness I experienced during my run a day prior. It all happened as it was intended to be, all part of God's plan. This entire journey is His plan. As I write these very words, I am unsure of what will be written next because I am not privy to His plan. I would love to contact a publisher. But how do you pitch a book that has no ending? How do you explain that you are living the book every day? How do you explain that your words are delivered by God, at will, on any given day and time?

It's a leap of faith.

Would you leap?

LET THERE BE PEACE ON EARTH

"Let there be peace on earth and let it begin with me." These are the words of a song that had been ringing in my ear. When I was a child, we would sing this in church. With the peace that has been surrounding me, it occurred to me that perhaps there was some truth to this song. The events that had been occurring around me had been pretty incredible, so incredible that the only explanation seems to be that God truly knows my every thought. I will do my very best to describe the most recent events in my life and you can be the judge.

My oldest daughter had been home from school sick and there is a bit of a story to go with our visit to the doctor's office. She and my six-year-old son were both sick this week. Neither one of them has mastered the art of a throat culture. But have any of us, really? With the mention of the throat culture, my son immediately went into panic mode, and the doctor made the decision not to culture his throat because he would be medicated anyway for a slight skin infection under his nose. The antibiotic would cover a potential strep throat. Next up was my eleven-year-old daughter. With anxiety being a small part of her personality and throat cultures being a trigger, I knew this would be difficult. Even so, I remained calm, so calm, as calm as the ocean without a wave. When the doctor mentioned the culture, my daughter immediately froze and went into panic mode. I remained calm. As the doctor tried to reassure her, her anxiety increased. As the anxiety increased, her behavior became like that of a toddler having a tantrum. It was very sad to see how she had no control of this. I remained calm. When the doctor was out of words, she looked at me mildly suggesting that we treat without the culture. I refused. With more coaxing, my daughter was at the peak of irrational behavior. The doctor seemed rattled, but I remained calm. With this, I winked at the doctor knowing that I would have my friend, God, help me with this. Upon the doctor leaving the room, I did not say a word; rather, I silently put my head in my hands, looked down, and asked the Holy Spirit to enter the room with an army of angels. Next I looked at my daughter, and at that moment, I remembered that I had a prayer for mental health on my Blackberry as I had just emailed it to a friend in need. I told my daughter and son that we were going to quiet ourselves and pray. My daughter, still unnerved, quieted herself and I recited the prayer:

> O lady of mental peace, mother of tranquility
> and mother of hope, look upon me in this time
> of my weakness and unrest.

Teach my searching heart to know that God's love for me is unchanging and unchangeable; and that true human love can only begin and grow by touching His love.

Let your gentle peace, which this world cannot give, be always with me. And, help me to bring this same peace into the lives of others.

Our lady of mental peace, pray for me!

Within moments, there was calmness. My daughter now had the ability to have a rational conversation about the throat culture. She admitted to wanting to do it but not feeling brave enough. She mentioned that she was upset that if she didn't go through with the culture, she feared I would be mad. I assured her that my love was unconditional, and when we walked out of the examining room, we would leave the whole situation behind us. I explained that she would have a clean slate. We discussed that in life there is darkness and light. And although she was having a dark moment, the light would come after she got the culture and felt proud of herself. She would also learn that in any tough situation, she could rely on God and make it through. She paused for a moment and said, "I think I can do this now, but can I sit on your lap?"

With the door opened a crack, I could see the nurses had been listening outside in the hallway. Naturally the nurse came in, discussed the culture, and assured my daughter she would do it quickly and was the best at it. My daughter tilted her head, opened her mouth, and the culture was completed without her flinching. When it was done, she said, "That wasn't bad at all."

We left and as promised, it was not discussed further. With sick children, doctor appointments, and bringing peace to a throat culture, I never took a moment to plan the logistics of the half-marathon.

Preparing for a half-marathon involves planning: making arrangements for children, packing for the weekend, finding accommodations, and coordinating schedules with friends. There were many things that could go awry especially since my husband, a high school coach, had a game, and I, a math tutor, worked on Saturdays. I decided to just let the day unfold because I had faith it would be perfect. And as I thought, it occurred without a hitch. After two phone calls, I landed a place to stay with friends. The miracle of this was that, in past years, we had called about ten hotels to be told, "No room in the inn!" The next call confirmed that a babysitter was available to stay over at my house with my three children.

As planned, we were on the road and arrived at my friend's house in plenty of time to make a six fifteen dinner reservation. At dinner, I discovered that the church I was planning to attend did not have a Mass at the time I thought. With urgency sprinkled with panic, I grabbed my Blackberry to search for churches in the area. I was not met with much success. Within moments everyone's iPhones and Blackberries were activated in a quest to find a church. I had to attend Mass. There was no way I was going to miss it for I had to complete a novena[10] that concluded with attending Mass on Divine Mercy Sunday. I had many prayer requests riding on this! When we couldn't find a Mass and my friends couldn't understand my passion, I began to think why can't anyone understand my burning desire to attend Mass? With this question and my feelings of disappointment, I began to realize that perhaps my spirituality, my faith, and my union with God were different from most. While ultimately wonderful, in the moment it was a difficult pill to swallow. During this moment I excused myself to call my editor. Shortly after speaking with her, I landed a church one mile down the road with a 7:30 p.m. Mass in Portuguese! Upon walking into the church, I saw a mural of the vision that my novena was based on. God was with me. After Mass, I approached a statue of Mary in the front of the church with Caroline whom I had trained for the upcoming race. Keeping with our routine, we prayed in front of the Blessed Mother, and asked her to be with us on race day.

Typically, with the arrival of race day came an energy. (Good Lord, I had enough energy these days I surely did not need anymore.) The energy is usually one of excitement; it's a fun, exciting, nervous energy. Yet for me, this time, there was not one bit of nervous energy; rather, there was an amazing calm. As odd as that sounds, that's the best way to describe it. When Caroline woke up, I could hear the nervous energy swirling around the guest bedroom where she slept with her mom. I heard her stating how her back was in pain. With that, I offered some sports cream for her mom to apply to the base of her back. After the cream was applied, she was still in pain. Before we left for the race, noting that she was nervous, I grabbed my

Blackberry and we prayed the mental health prayer. In addition, I asked her to put her hand on the spot where she was experiencing the pain. With that, I touched her back and silently prayed, asking the Holy Spirit to be with Caroline during her run and I asked God to alleviate the pain.

As we made our way to the start, we encountered many people along the way. Because I am a magnet for people with nervous energy, they all found me like a misplaced fish searching for water. So, here I was talking to strangers about this nervous energy and reassuring them about their training, and the beauty of the cool, crisp, sunny day. The irony of the whole situation was that all of them would probably pass me on the course while I enjoyed the journey. For my body wasn't made to run, but it is something I enjoy doing.

Ready, set, go! The gun sounded and we were off. Within moments of the start, I found two girls running in front of me talking about the Jesus prayer. Amen, I thought. This was going to be a fabulous run. As I looked at the back of their t-shirts, I see as clear as day the words, "I am running for... the Wellness Community." So, within moments of the start of this glorious race, I was reminded of my vision of a spiritual wellness center. As we continued to run, I noted a quote on the back of another runner's shirt. "I can do all things with Christ who strengthens me" (Philippians 4:13). How about that?

During the run, I noticed peace had hit my running. I had my wind, my legs were feeling great, and I was finally feeling like the girl who could run at her former pace. I was running like a girl who had been set free by the truth. I was finally back. On the other hand, Caroline seemed to be struggling with a knee that was hurting her, a need to go to the bathroom, and an inability to get in a running zone. I silently, yes, *silently*, supported her every step. Sometimes side by side, other moments a pace in front. Although I knew I could have run right on ahead, it was far more rewarding to sacrifice my running time to be supportive to a young girl who was running her very first half-marathon. The ironic thing was that at the beginning of the race, I had told her to run her pace because I was unsure if I would be able to keep up with her. So, here I was supporting a girl the way I would have dreamed of being supported, when I struggled with my running, after recovering from a surgery. To give compassion to Caroline was God's greatest gift to me. That, and knowing that my running groove was back, was enough for me.

As we approached mile 9, it was obvious that Caroline's knee was really hurting. We stopped and stretched. Knowing that her mom was spectating on this mile, I was anxious for Caroline to see her, for there is nothing like seeing your loving mom. Bingo! There she was at mile 9.5. We embraced, posed for pictures, and carried on. With Caroline still hurting, we saw *out of nowhere*, a priest walking on the street with his collar on and a Bible in hand. I looked at Caroline and said, "That might as well have been Jesus Himself!" We laughed and with that a young guy who was walking giggled at us, took his cross out from under his shirt, and started running along side of us. I said to him, "Come on, Jesus carried a cross. You can finish this last part." He smiled. We all put our music back on and we ran silently next to each other.

Approaching mile 10, I noticed a tightness in my legs but kept on going. At mile 11, while my legs started cramping, Caroline said to me, "I just got in my groove." I laughed to myself because I was starting to hurt and I could have used her to keep me going right then. I told her my legs were tight and we got to mile 11.5. Feeling like I might have to slow down or walk, Caroline said, "Come on, we are so close." With that, I committed to not walking one step and doing whatever it took to finish running.

A natural distance came between Caroline and me. I was running out of the gas she had. I had her in sight the entire time as I was falling behind. We finished the race two minutes apart. My initial thought was, "Ughh, I ran step for step with you for 11.5 miles. How could you leave me in the end?" I dismissed the thought and replaced it with "Wow, I just trained a young girl to successfully complete a half-marathon as well as a spiritual journey." I felt proud. Caroline came up to me and said, "Sorry I ran ahead but I had to. I was in pain and got thoughts of not finishing. I had to sprint it out and get to the finish as fast as I could." At that moment, I realized that it wasn't about me and it is so much better when it's about someone else. One day, I will have a race that is all about me. This wasn't the one.

Arriving home, I received a text from Caroline that stated, "Thanks for the spiritual journey!" And one from her mom, Mary, "MJ, thank you for being a part of Caroline's journey. She couldn't have done it without you." After receiving these texts, I asked Caroline if she would like to end the journey with a prayer of thanksgiving in front of the Blessed Mother Statue. With that, Caroline came over to my house. We bought a potted mum plant, visited Mary, and thanked her for her support.

So there you have it.... "Let there be peace on earth and let it begin with me." Want to jump on the peace train?

EVERYDAY CHRISTIAN OR NOT?

As I rode this peace train I began to get frustrated. You may be thinking, "What was so frustrating about being on a peace train?" Well, I will do my very best to explain my frustration.

So I jumped on this peace train with nothing more than a leap of faith, a faith in God that I did not question. A faith that was so very strong. But how would you feel if you jumped onto a train where the destination was unknown, as are the stops along the way? You could not jump off because, if you tried, you'd get pulled back on, and by trying, you would be walking away from God's call. To further explain, it should be known that I am a person of action. I will make a goal, formulate a plan, execute the plan, and, normally, be very successful in the process and the end result. Clearly, I have God to thank for that. So here I was, a girl with a calling, who would like to make a plan and get this show on the road. Instead, I was on the express train to Leap-of-Faithville, without a map or a tour guide, who had traveled this path before.

While on this train, I tried very hard to maintain my tutoring business, a family, and millions of thoughts that came into my head on a daily basis. When I felt like I wanted to jump off and rebel, I was only drawn more to my computer to write a story that I was unsure of the ending or the outcome. Would these words ever be read by anyone? This train ride was a test of mental strength and patience. However, soon I would have to admit that the positive outcomes that had come with this energy were worth every bit of the frustration.

I was left to wonder, "Am I an everyday Christian?" Didn't everyone help others with a minute's notice? Didn't everyone feel another's pain the way I did? Didn't we all have a special relationship with God that was unique to us? Didn't everybody try to lead a Christ-like life? This was all so confusing for me, because in my home it was the norm. It was what I have grown up with my entire life, how I was raised as a child and as an adult. The same "norm" existed in my house now. My husband is one of the kindest souls I have ever encountered in my whole life. So great, "Yeah!" to me and this peace train existence that I am living. The reality was, while it was an honor, it was also becoming a pain in the caboose.

I was beginning to realize that not everyone saw the world as I did. I was so very happy to be an agent of change, but I would have loved a little direction and I was growing impatient as I waited, for this was not my style. I loved a challenge and I would sprint to it. I was not even jogging right now. So here I was, a girl with "fashion first" as a motto in new running sneakers, a great running outfit, at the starting line, and the gun was not sounding. For the love of God, let's start this race. Really, how patient could one girl be?

As I wrote and wrote and wrote, my children were aware of this new obsession. My son said to me the other day, "So, Ma, you writing your chirrch (he was six and hadn't mastered "r" controlled words yet) book again? Is it about God? Are you going to give it to a priest? Is it a chapter book? Does it have a cover?" His energy was almost as contagious as mine. He then upped the ante and asked if I could read it to him. So he sat on my lap and I read the prior day's chapter, which mentioned him. He asked me, "How is this about God?" I explained how God was part of our everyday actions. I recalled how we had said a prayer in the doctor's office to help us. He hesitated and said, "Oh, I get it. So it's like when we talk to God in our heads." At that very moment, I realized that if the sole (or soul) purpose of my writing was to bring an awareness of God's constant presence to a child, then, "Amen". At the same time though, there was a little part of me that would love to sit on the Oprah Winfrey show and be interviewed about it. A girl can dream.

Rewinding to last evening and what I saw when I walked into my son's bedroom, I had tucked him into bed, and moments later he asked me to come into his room because I forgot to shut off the light. I walked in very quietly thinking that he might be falling asleep. As I walked in he did not see me, but I saw him. He was kneeling with his eyes shut and his hands in the prayer position praying. I said nothing. When he became aware of my presence, he remained still and continued to pray with his eyes shut. Upon completing his prayers, he got under his covers. Not a word was spoken between us. I kissed him good night and that vision will stay with me forever.

This morning I awoke, and as I tried to make a very difficult decision – yoga or running, I hesitated and thought about a friend, who needed an ear to listen and a shoulder to lean on. So I put a call out, and I made a coffee date instead. She came over and talked while I listened. Didn't everyone do this? Don't we all put our lives on hold to help someone? After an hour of talking I saw a little relief in her face. I decided that I needed to go to daily Mass to pray for her. In going to Mass for a friend's intention, ironically, I received more than I was there to give. After Mass, another grace-filled moment occurred when I had a meaningful conversation with Father Neutral that affirmed a moment in this journey.

So as I closed today's writing, I realized that as much as I had wanted to stick to my plan for my day, it was God's plan that allowed me to get it all in: go to Mass, run three miles, food shop, cook dinner, pick up the kids from school, and work. I realized the beauty of this journey; the beauty of growing closer to my family; the beauty of understanding that in surrendering to God's Will, not mine, He was going to change my life in a profound way. With this realization I decided I was staying on this express train where the destination was unknown even though my patience was growing thin. I will, however, have you ponder this: Are you an everyday Christian?

CHRIST
BE MY LIGHT

As I sat in the church writing in a journal, I asked why, for this journey was a bit easier sitting at my computer and writing my thoughts at lightning speed, using spell-check, because I am a mathematician at heart, and not a spelling bee queen. So here I sat with pencil in hand, in front of the altar as I tried to explain to my son that God had called me to be in His house. You see, if I hadn't come, my day would have gotten very dark. As a matter of fact when I chose not to write and put it off to another day, the darkness came. It came in the form of thoughts – thoughts that I was a freak (the Jesus had been subtracted from the equation) on this journey. I was such a freak that I struggled to simply find a priest who could guide me on this journey. It left me with the question: "Who will this priest be?" My faith made me realize that perhaps there may be more than one priest for this job.

Before I bring you to a flash back of last week, I must take a moment to explain the here and now and how I was led to the church with my journal. Out of nowhere, I was flooded with negative thoughts. These thoughts came shortly after I sent a text to my editor, questioning the presence of a priest as a spiritual director on the journey (as I wrote this, I was listening to *Jesus Freak* music and the words "don't give up" were playing...interesting). I stated that a priest would keep evil away. Shortly after that text, I was flooded with negative thoughts. Knowing that I had been encouraged to write in a journal in the church by Father Reserved, she had the perfect wisdom to suggest that I should go to the church. In addition, my Jesus freak sister, had advised me to listen to Christian music, because it would immediately send evil spirits running for the hills. As I gathered my journal, my prayer to St. Michael (the angel who drove Satan and his legions from heaven and plunged them into the depths of hell), my son, and rosary beads for him, I jumped in my car. As I got in the car, I blasted a CD that I had from a parish retreat I had attended. The funny thing was that this CD had been lost until the day before. I was upset that I didn't have it, but that Sunday, a voice inside me told me exactly where to look, and in one shot, I found it after I had searched high and low for it in previous weeks. So with music blaring like I was at a Bruce Springsteen concert, I drove my car to the church like an ambulance on a call for an exorcism. And, that was how, and why, this chapter started in a journal.

As I had stated in my previous chapter, my patience was growing thin. While I was ready to move to the next phase of this journey, I felt like I was on a treadmill in the cool down mode. Clearly, this was not my style. I had full understanding that on any journey there would be a learning curve, and for me, I must learn patience. Trust me, I was trying.

Last week I felt like I had questions that weren't being answered, and as I struggled, I became frustrated. While I was busy bringing peace to others and reaching out to the point where my life was on hold, no one was reaching out to me. It was so frustrating, that it brought me to the point of tears, like the water that was falling on that rainy day.

I took the frustration to church with hopes to find peace, but there was none. I was called to write but was not obeying. I took my frustration to the cemetery. I have not mentioned the fact that in my life I lost my dad at age eight, a quite fabulous brother at age nineteen, and another equally fabulous brother at age twenty-six (I think twenty-six. This death was so very painful that I am unsure of my age. It's how the brain works, blocking out horrible memories). In addition, my husband and I lost a baby at twenty-four weeks of pregnancy. I also lost three grandparents within two years of losing my dad. Needless to say, I had many angels to visit at the cemetery. On this rainy day, it seemed appropriate to go to the place where it was most fitting to cry and leave the tears behind.

As I was on my way to the cemetery, my phone sounded and in came a text from a girl who I had been called to bring peace. She too had lost a brother and I was well aware of the pain that comes with that loss. The irony was that she was also a friend of one of my brothers. Her timing was surreal. I was crying a river, and I could not find one grave that I was looking for. With all the angels I have just mentioned, the probability was pretty high of me landing one! I walked back to the car and tried to collect my thoughts, as it was raining, and I was now shivering in a wet shirt and no coat. Via text, I explained to my friend where I was, and she remained with me by way of text, the entire time I was in the cemetery.

As I struggled with the fact that I could not find my brothers' grave site, within moments the words came to me, "under small tree, to the right." I got out of the car, walked to the tree and there it was. Seeing my brothers' names evoked tears and I let them out. Next stop: Dad. It was easy to find my dad once I located my brothers because his grave formed a right triangle with my grandparents being the third side. I followed the diagonal. No Dad. I retraced my steps, no Dad. I broadened the search while I stopped to text my friend. With this distraction, I realized that I was standing on a grave. When I realized and thought that I was being disrespectful, with a quick prayer of forgiveness, I looked down to see Joseph and Angelina Cavalieri, my grandparents. I prayed, cried, and walked back to find my dad. The rain came down harder and I shivered more, so I walked back to the car knowing I would visit my dad and baby another day.

Upon arriving home I emailed my Jesus freak sister. I explained my bad day and how I found it unfair that while I helped others, I felt like no one was helping me. With this, I landed the perfect advice. Number 1: Go to confession because God is present in the sacraments. Number 2: Get to a perpetual adoration chapel, pose a question in the Lord's presence, and sit in silence and let the thoughts come to you. His answer would come in the form of thoughts. In addition, my editor sent me an email at the exact same time. Exact. I finally got peace in addition to a plan to go to the chapel with my editor and my cemetery texting friend. And boy, did the Lord talk! Buckle up for His messages:

> Peace…it surrounds you
> You are bringing it to…
> Amy, Jane, Kerrie, Frank, Jamie, Joe, Jillian, John, Jack
> (I did not know who five of these people were)
> Change is coming sooner than you think
> There will be an appearance
> Keep writing
> Come back
> Be with your friends
> Thank you for accepting the journey
> Sorry for your bad day
> Get to confession

How about that? Because when you are on a journey, there are lessons to be learned, I stopped and reflected about what I had learned. As always, in darkness there was light. When I was having a dark moment, a girl to whom I was delivering peace became the light that I needed. Darkness and light became one. In addition, I realized that perhaps I needed to be less independent and learn to depend on others. When I depended on people like my sister and my editor, I found peace.

Next stop: Confession.

In an attempt to find a spiritual director, I found that I was struggling with approaching a priest to have a conversation. This was very odd, for I am a person who can talk about anything with anyone at any given time. This struggle made me think. With that analysis came answers as to why I had priest avoidance.

First, I feared that they would minimize what was going on and would give me a response like "You are already leading a good Christian life, blah-blah-blah…" and I was not interested in hearing that. While I understood that I walk the walk, it was time to make it on a larger scale. Second, there was a chance they might think I was nuts, and third, if they did validate what was happening, it would truly become real.

With prayers for guidance for the right priest and a conversation with my editor who, like my sister, had wisdom that I did not have, a confirmation came that Father Reserved was the priest to approach. I learned that he would be hearing confessions on Saturday. I had seen him the week before in confession and I had been so moved by the experience. I had thought for sure that he was the one. With high expectations of this meeting, I had great hope of entering the next phase of this journey. Great hope.

This great hope turned into great frustration when I attended confession and I was not met with the words I had been expecting. In my mind, I had prayed, had already had a positive confession encounter with this very same priest before, and had researched that he would be in the confessional a second time. Because it was "confession," I had the courage to speak freely and had reached out to a priest who I did not know very well. In fairness to the priest, he could not have known the work that I had done to get to this point. He was helpful by suggesting that I try to write out my thoughts in a journal while in the presence of the Lord. He advised praying and thinking about who I thought would be the proper choice for my spiritual director. In my head, I had felt he was the one, and knew I would have to re-address this. I told him that I would meet his suggestion of writing in a journal with reluctance. He said that I should stay away from the computer, and by coming to the church, I would be forced to set aside specific time so that the writing wouldn't consume my day. He wasn't getting it, but I was gracious, and *not*, all at the same time, when I jokingly said, "Thanks for nothing" with a smirky smile on my face.

Arriving home more frustrated than you can imagine, I unloaded on my husband who would have done anything to make me feel better. It occurred to me to email the priest and explain how I had reached my conclusion to go to him through prayer. When I went to the church website, I could not find an email address for the man who suggested I write in a journal – yes, very funny to you, but not to me at that moment. I complained to my editor and to my sister. I put it to rest until the next day, Sunday.

With Sunday, came Mass and more prayers about leading me to the right spiritual director. After Mass I saw all the priests outside. I felt as if I was the radius of a circle, and each priest was on the outer edge of my circle, for I could walk in any direction and approach whomever I wanted. It was exactly what I had been praying for − a natural situation to approach a priest for a conversation. Here was my moment to tell my guy that he is the one. Oh, the relief! But as fate would have it, a rather large-bottomed senior citizen cut me off and blocked the goal. For the love of God! What nerve! I wanted to cry. Feeling dejected, I went home and explained the situation to my Jesus freak sister and I texted my editor. My sister suggested writing a note. How brilliant. Write a note to the guy who suggested archaic journal writing. With that suggestion I wrote a witty note and drove directly to the rectory with it. I was relieved.

The next morning, I started the day at 8:00 a.m. Mass with my stepdad's health as my prayer intention. He had a heart condition and I had been concerned about him. After a visit with him and my mom, I came home to get a call from the priest. I was met with hesitation, reservation, and a commitment from him to pray and discern if he was the guy for the job. Although I understood, frustration continued to mount. With the frustration came dark thoughts and me again disobeying my calling to write… well, we know where this was leading. Are you seeing a pattern? The battle between good and evil was starting. However, I had learned to depend on my editor who advised me to pick up my journal and get to church. As I was battling the thoughts, I realized that my cross had not been around my neck because I had taken it off to take a shower. With that, I put my cross on, grabbed my journal and my son, and ran out the door.

My son said, "Ma, why we going to chirrch? You already went this morning." I said that we had to go so we could talk to God. He was relieved when he heard it wasn't Mass and he perked up. "So we are like just going to sit and talk to Him like I do before I go to sleep?" I confirmed his thought. "So like did He call you and tell you to come?"

I said, "Kind of. He is calling me to be there."

My son replied, "Then let's go…but, Mom, is it illegal to bring jelly beans?" I initially had to use the jelly beans as a bribe because he was not happy about going to church. I reassured him that he could eat the candy.

When we arrived at church, I was at peace and happy to sit in the last pew. My son said to me, "Hey, Ma, I want to sit all the way in the front row." With that we walked to the front of the church. I taught him how to genuflect. I sat, he knelt, and said, "Ma, when I pray, I kneel." With that I knelt. He looked at me out of the corner of his eye. "Ma, I also close my eyes." With that I closed my eyes. We prayed, and after a short period of time, we both sat. I wrote and he ate jelly beans. While I was writing he stated, "Ma, how do you know what to write?" I explained that I didn't know what I was going to write, but that when the words came to me I would write them down. He said, "So like God gives you the words?"

I said, "Yes, He does."

He said, "So like you don't know the ending yet?" I told him that was correct. Wisdom…my son got it. He also asked when I was going to give my "church book" to the priest. I didn't have the heart to tell him that I had tried but it hadn't been accepted at this point.

When you are searching for an answer, is Christ your light?

LESSONS LEARNED

Going to the chapel seemed to be the next thing on the "to do" list for this journey. It seemed that every bit of advice my Jesus freak sister had been doling out was spot-on. Yes, spot-on. So I contacted my editor and decided to take a trip to the chapel and do exactly what my sister suggested, for I was not interested in a bad day – not today, not tomorrow, not ever. What I had also learned was that when I was not in contact with my editor when I needed to be, the darkness would roll in.

Struggling with the question "What priest would accompany me on this journey?", I laced up my sneakers to go for a run. While I was running, I listened to my church music and was getting into a groove. Then I saw the priest, Father Neutral, whom I had reached out to on several occasions. I threw my hands in the air and gave a wave, thinking, "He is so not the guy for this job." As I continued running, I paused for a moment and texted my editor that very thought. Now as I write this I think, "May God bless her and her patience for dealing with me." At that moment I don't even think that I could have dealt with myself and the thoughts that were flying into my head like the Concorde flying to London. As soon as I texted that bold statement, the song "Open My Eyes, Lord" started playing: "Open my eyes, Lord, help me to see your face…" Well, after hearing that song, I grabbed my phone and texted my editor, saying, "Shoot, he *can't* be the one." I continued running and thought that perhaps my friend God had taught me a lesson on humility. I swallowed the humility pill and kept running.

I realized I needed to go to the chapel, and while hanging out with my friend, God, I would pose the question about good old Father Neutral. Within moments of a call to my editor to request the chapel express bus, she arrived, and we drove to the chapel. As soon as I opened the door, before I could even sit down in a chair, I heard, "Father Neutral *is* the one, not the only one…" Wow, was I surprised, yet not. My friend God is very chatty about many things, but it came right back to the fact that He has known my every thought and was aware of my frustration with this situation, but to have patience…yes, patience. Clearly, I was coming to understand that the reason God had chosen my editor to be my companion on this journey was to help teach me that, because this chick had the patience of a saint. For starters, dealing with me and my special "gifts of the Holy Spirit" was no easy task as all I wanted to do was write and talk and text and go to the chapel and be at Mass and write and talk and text. Are you getting it? I was a royal pain and she was by my side every moment in the most peaceful, supportive manner with crazy patience. Seriously, she's like Mother Teresa. God was a good man to match me with her. He knew what He was doing.

Besides this priestly patience revelation, there were many other chapel whispers from my friend, God, but I will stick to a few: "Every thought. I know it, every single one... Aware that you are annoyed with the priests. Patience... Happy, so happy, you are writing... Publish... Jesus freak... Very funny... Saint... Family of saints... Kerrie you must see her (my sister-in-law, wife of my brother who died twenty-two years ago)... Chris is on the path with Father Reserved... No, Father Neutral... Happy now?"

Well, I left the chapel with a supersized humility pill that I had to swallow. I felt like I had been eating humility pills like they were candy...all for the love of God!

Next Lesson: Obedience.

The next day, I was exhausted from having processed all these thoughts at lightning speed, awakened in the middle of the night, and thinking about finding time to write the next chapter, all while being aware of and respecting the call. At one o'clock in the afternoon, I was called to take a nap by my friend, God. Having never been a "napper," I found it odd. But, with respect to the call and feeling overwhelming exhaustion, I listened and went upstairs. As I crawled into bed, I was thinking what time should I set my alarm. I heard, "One forty-five." With that, I set my alarm and settled into the warmth of my bed. Just as I was drifting into a drooling sound sleep, I awoke and heard, "Get journal and go to church." Well, I was not happy at all with this statement, but because I was not interested in having a dark day, I was obedient and did as I was told. Arriving at the church I found three women who worked there, one of whom is my Mother Teresa-like editor. In addition to anger, I was cringing because I was not interested in this public display of my writing. So I sat in the last pew with my head down as I wrote the following:

> So here I sit in the back of the church writing, not wanting to do this, wondering why I have been called. I am following every, every, command. I am aware that You know my every thought. I am very surprised that I find no silence in the church. I am annoyed that I am here but I am complying with a request that I can make no sense of...none...not one ounce of sense.

I was told, "Silence..." I stopped writing and listened to the sound of the running water of the baptismal font. I resumed writing.

> I have listened to the homily. I am including others I suppose by a public display of my writing in church. I have reached out for guidance with no response. I have shared my/Your thoughts with my mom. Complete obedience. Complete.

I heard, "Listen...Just listen...You can go now. Thanks for coming. It was a lesson on obedience. Amen."

I walked back to my car in awe, complete and total awe, that this had just happened. I opened the car door to hear the sound of my cell phone alarm going off because it was one forty-five. So there you have it…my friend God threw down the plan and I obeyed. I guess I get an A+ for obedience today.

When I arrived home, I got ready to work in my home, as a private math tutor. Teaching that afternoon was difficult as I was preoccupied with the day's events. I was yearning to go to the chapel and I couldn't get there fast enough. Finally when my work was complete, I went to the chapel with a different friend. The chapel whisperings that I heard that night were incredible – totally incredible!

I will summarize as best I can: As I write this, I am still in complete awe, as I was completely honored that such a sacred moment happened to me, an everyday, Aisle 7 ShopRite girl, who was *never* an outward Jesus freak. Clearly, I was a closet one and the door was now being opened. Amen, I say.

So, there I was sitting in the chapel with a friend who had lost her brother, and needed as much peace as I could bring her. She had been a friend of my angel brother Chris, who was as special and as beautiful as the Pieta[11]. I listened. I felt my brother Chris' presence as he started talking – yes, wild! While this was happening, as excited as I was, because I had waited twenty-two years for this to happen, I was also as calm as I would have been throwing back a beer with him. So there I sat in the presence of the Lord, and listened to my brother's every word.

While he affirmed that my chapel companion and my editor were super and fabulous for they were both his friends, he begged me, and I mean *begged me*, to get in touch with his wife because she needed peace. The funny thing was that we already had plans to meet – not really funny – all a part of a much bigger plan. We expressed how much we missed each other and he confirmed that I was being called by God and told me to follow the call. He explained that the chapel conversations were going to become more of a flowing conversation because I was more open to the gift, and that I was the luckiest girl in the world to have it…so *lucky*. He spoke of my mom and my brother. Chris told me he is with my grandparents, my dad, and my angel baby. Yes, incredible.

Next, my other brother Paul, spoke to me in the most heartfelt manner. For anyone reading this that did not know Paul, he was nothing but heart. He was the biggest mush, the kindest soul, with compassion so deep, even for a flea on the cat. This guy was the life of the party, a truly loveable soul. We were so very close until his illness hit and he took his life. His death was so very devastating for me. No death is easy to accept but suicide is a whole different category. So, when Paul started talking and told me he was so sorry that he left me, I was overcome with shock that this was happening, yet calm while in the moment. Here I was sitting chatting with my brother as he explained every detail surrounding the end of his short life. God knew I needed to hear from both of my brothers and He made this happen. I could feel my brother's embrace. I could feel his sorrow and remorse. I felt every ounce of his love and I knew he felt mine.

Finally, I heard from my father and my editor's dad. My dad was quiet yet proud. He was in awe of my journey and let me know that he was with my angel baby. Now, hearing from my editor's dad was something. For starters, I have never met him. He identified himself, and let me tell you, this guy had an intense presence. I am telling you, when he talked, you listened the first time. You did not blink and you followed the plan he threw down. He was firm, yet comforting. He was gentle, yet strong. This guy was something. He was the type of person you were drawn to. You just wanted to be in his presence.

At the end of this amazing chapel visit, my friend God stepped forward and said (buckle up because this is something), "You deserve this after an *obedient* day. Pray and go. Love you and your work. Pappa Ova and Outt" (funny but this is how I often sign my texts or e-mails to people).

I realized that I had just gotten to say the good-byes I never had. A heavenly angel friend of my editor that also had "spoken" to me in the chapel reminded me that it was not good-bye but hello forever. Are you in as much awe as I am?

Next Stop: Patience.

As I learned patience, I planned for my meeting with my church group. This was the meeting that was coming together that I spoke of in an earlier chapter. I will include the essay that I ended up presenting that night, which came to me in no time.

When God calls, you need to answer for great things will come. This is not a call that should go to voicemail or the in-box for a delayed reply. It is a call that you need to answer and take immediate action. It is a call that can change your life forever. It is a call worth taking.

For me it started with a faith I never knew I had. My faith was like a given in a geometry proof. Without the given, a conclusion could never result. So it seemed only natural that everyone walked around with the same "given" in their geometric composition. An awakening for me is that not every one has this thing called faith. What a shock for me. It seemed as routine as breathing. I came to this realization about four years ago when I was attending a church retreat. Here I was in a room with wonderful women called together by their faith. As the conversation unfolded, I began to realize that what I had was special, that not everyone in the room shared the great faith that I had.

It was at that moment that I made the rather arrogant statement that I still chuckle at today...

I feel like I am on the AP (advanced placement) track of faith.

As the words came out of my mouth, I realized my arrogance and wanted to die, for I felt I had just insulted everyone in the room *or* I might have made them feel that there was something out there so great that they needed to acquire. But I continued:

At that moment, my journey continued. A journey that I didn't even know was happening. With this awareness I realized that I had to take it up a notch but I didn't know how. I continued to be that girl. The girl who would listen, console, counsel, love, and try to live a life that mimicked Jesus' way. I believe in leading by example. All of a sudden listening to someone's problems in aisle 7 of ShopRite for twenty-five minutes while my shopping wasn't getting done, meeting a friend to comfort her over the loss of her brother, or skipping a yoga class because a friend needed to talk, just didn't seem like it was enough. Something started happening, I had this tugging feeling inside me. A voice kept saying there is more. The voice kept getting louder and louder. It became so loud that I was distracted. It was like a magnet that pulled me into church EVERY day for daily Mass. It pulled me to my computer to write, and write and write and write. I saw God in everything; He became a part of my every thought, and I felt like I was a part of His. This call was as loud as a siren going off saying, "Let's go, it is time to get started!" But here is the problem, what am I supposed to be doing?

So here I am with an open heart, an open mind, and a willingness to serve God and travel down a path with an uncertain outcome. A peace bubble surrounds me. This peace bubble has the feeling of the greatest peace you could possibly imagine. It is as peaceful as the silence of a mother cradling her child, a calm serene peace that touches the core of your soul; a peace that can only come from God's tender embrace; a peace that can barely be put into words. Anyone in my path has been positively affected. The examples of this peace are as long as a grocery list for a homeless person. The forgiveness that I have for life's hurts is extraordinary. I have a willingness to forgive all, and love all, unconditionally. The energy I feel is sometimes too overwhelming even for me to comprehend. It has become more than obvious that God is leading me down a path. It is clear that you are part of it. For if you weren't, this essay would not have been in my head and none of you would have responded to the call of an email.

In conclusion, God is talking to all of us. Do not hit mute, delete or leave it in the "inbox" too long. It is time to listen to this call and respond in a way that is most fit for each of us.

Amen

I was nervous to read it, which was so not me. But as I read and the girls listened very intently, they seemed to be craving for more. I read the scene and I started explaining this journey where the destination was not known. Some seemed riveted, others indifferent. I talked, they listened, we prayed, we bonded. We all agreed to Friday morning prayer at my house, 6:00 a.m. for those who worked, and 8:45 a.m. for others. I had thought we would start the following week, but they asked to come back the following day for more. How about that? I would spread Christianity one person at a time if I had to. Clearly, this journey was contagious. Our prayer was beautiful the next morning. It was exactly how it was intended to be: five Christian women gathered in a kitchen praying for silent intentions and the intentions of the journey. Beautiful, absolutely, beautiful. I could feel God smile.

Next stop: A delivery of peace.

I reflected on my brother Chris' words and contacted my sister-in-law when I noticed that the date we had scheduled to meet (a month prior) was not going to work. In reflecting back, there was no coincidence that we were meant to get together. She responded within a twenty-four hour period and we made plans to meet that very day, a Saturday. I was excited and anxious all at the same time. I wanted to be a non-tearful peace giver. The only problem was, I became aware of the fact, that it might be impossible to keep a dry eye as I sat across from a girl who captured my very special brother's heart, and he, my friends, was a special soul. So special, it's hard to describe. He was the guy who always had a smile on his face, the guy whom everyone loved, the guy who would stay up until midnight studying science with me, his sixth-grade sister, while he had high school exams, the guy who would help his kid sister with college accounting courses with the patience of a saint. He was the guy whose death left a void in a kid sister's heart that could never be filled, but who left her with his ever-present presence. Bottom line, the guy was as rare as a book no longer printed. Hence, this was not an easy task.

After the chapel whispers from my brothers, my dad, and my editor's father and friend, a sort of spiritual "team" was formed, making the car ride interesting. They were the spiritual team that was to coach us during this journey. It was very fitting, because my editor's dad had a reputation of being one of the town's best coaches, and this was a job he knew well. So as I got in the car, I felt their presence. It was very comical. I even sent a text to my editor about it and she asked if they were buckled in! Their presence remained with me throughout the dinner with my sister-in-law. While at the dinner, I shared the message that my brother had given me and had begged me to deliver. I am still unsure of how it was received. But at the dinner when my sister-in-law discussed how she used to have dreams that were like visits from my brother, I was happy for her. However, she said that she hadn't had those dreams in a while and she missed them. Out of nowhere, I was prompted with such confidence and conviction to say, "No worries, you will have one of those dreams within twelve days." My sister-in-law looked puzzled and asked how I knew this. I told her I had a very strong feeling. We agreed that she was to let me know if this happened.

So for six hours we had dinner. We talked, we laughed, we loved. While I "felt" my brother's presence, Kerrie missed his presence in the most desperate way. There was profound sadness. The kind of sadness that hurts to see. I was so happy to have reconnected with Kerrie because peace was delivered in just one meeting. So, as my brother *desperately* requested, and as I desired to, I kept the communication flowing to the point where I would see her again in six days and I couldn't wait!

Next stop: In darkness there is light.

After that, however, a feeling of sadness came over me. A sadness so deep that it brought darkness to me the next day – a darkness I couldn't escape. The sadness came from several sources: a broken heart caused by re-opening a twenty-two year-old wound, a birthday that passed for my angel baby who could have been, anxiety that was not mine but had a paralyzing effect on its owner and myself, and an inability to serve as a volunteer at a church gathering. To explain the emotion attached to this day, I have included an email that I wrote to my editor back then.

Subject: The darkest day yet.

Today it is so dark I fear that light will never come… Never. The devil has entered this house and will not leave. He is here in so many forms that I am afraid this journey is going to come to a screeching halt and how sad that will be. As I write this, your dad's team is swarming and trying to comfort me…

As I try to piece back together my heart that had to relive every hurt I have experienced, I need silence from a man who is incapable of giving me that because my job is to soothe him. After twenty-one years of doing this, I am out of compassion, kindness, and words. I have no words for a man who could die a death from anxiety. Each time I put back a piece of my shattered heart, he pulls two more pieces out. His anxiety is killing both of us. My independence is being smothered by anxiety; he is extinguishing my bright light. I cannot lean on him nor do I want to. I want to approach this with the only way I know how…with independence and strength while all he wants is co-dependence that will cause me to drown in his anxiety. I am broken and need to piece together my broken spirit, and while doing this, I am unavailable to be his life raft… for if I try to be the life raft, I will drown. Where is my lifeline?

This has been a mean, sad, and dark day on a path I didn't choose. May God and St. Michael be with me at this very moment. Amen.

I sent this email to my editor at 3:32 p.m., knowing that she was having a very busy day with her son's Confirmation and probably feeling the Holy Spirit's presence and bright light, while I was dying a slow death of darkness.

I muddled through the day, took a trip to the cemetery with my husband and children, and then decided to sleep it off, and so I crawled into bed without eating dinner. I awoke around 10:00 p.m. to the sound of a text from my editor who was to save me. She offered to take me to the chapel and I told her to give me ten minutes in order to get up and get dressed.

On the way to the chapel we discussed how my sister-in-law was sad…very sad. I expressed that I felt grave concern for her. This feeling was confirmed in the chapel by both of my brothers. I also learned that I had to resolve all my hurts in order to continue on this journey. The ride home was filled with unrest. I couldn't get the vision of my brother Chris' sad eyes out of my head. He seemed sick with worry. It seemed as if there was a situation that needed immediate attention and he wanted me to devise a plan to stop an accident waiting to happen. The feeling in the car on the ride home was one of despair, worry, and fear. I couldn't shake the effects of my brother's presence. I was prompted by him to send my sister-in-law one of my writings. Since I had learned obedience and passed with an A+, upon saying good-bye to my editor with reluctance, for she was my only peace, I entered my house and went downstairs to my office. I prided myself with the fact that my office always had an aura of positive energy. I was hopeful I would feel the comfort of that when I entered. In contrast, I felt the exact opposite.

It was as if I couldn't even walk in. The energy had changed and I felt as if I was being knocked down by a tsunami-like wave and, if I fell down, I would never recover. With that feeling, I left my office and sent a text to my editor, stating, "The energy in my office has changed." With that she asked if I wanted her to come back, to which I replied, "Yes. Immediately!" I waited on my front porch for her with complete fear and anxiety in my heart, a fear that I cannot describe, a fear that could cause one to buckle at the knees and I felt that was happening to me. In all my years of knowing my editor, I have never ever seen such fierce determination as I had that very night. She reached into her purse and grabbed two strands of rosary beads as if they were weapons of mass destruction. She stepped into my office as if she was Rocky Balboa delivering the final blow to Apollo Creed. I have never witnessed anything like it. Never. With that, I entered behind her, and we prayed the rosary on my couch as I cried in fear of the darkness that had entered my home. It was at this moment, I knew that my editor was my protector, my shield, a person that would always have my back. Always. I have never felt anything like this in my entire life. It also occurred to me that she was starting to understand how dark my days could get. Upon completing the rosary, the darkness was lifted. Even as I write this, I cannot believe what went on that night in my office, the feeling of protection, and the feeling that light beat darkness.

Next Lesson: Independence/Dependence.

On this journey, I had realized that when I was brought to my breaking point and I could take no more, darkness rolled in. In darkness there was learning, and with each lesson learned, came the brightest of bright in the following days. I had learned to depend on my editor. I had learned that my very independent nature was both a blessing and a curse and I needed to find the balance. I was finding it. By learning to depend on my editor, I had also learned to depend on my friend, God. What a beautiful thing!

On this very bright day, I had a meeting scheduled with Father Reserved, and what a meeting it was. We sat, he asked questions and listened. Clearly, he was interviewing me to make sure I was not some nut job with no basis for my thought process. I could tell the meeting was going well when he gave me a homework assignment to read books. In addition, he said that while he was going away for five weeks, he would be happy to chat with me when he returned. Well, how about that? I could depend on a priest if I chose to! Clearly, I passed this test. But here is the clincher, as I was leaving his office, I ran into the other priest I had reached out to for guidance. He offered to meet with me the following day. I jumped at the opportunity.

I spoke to my editor and devised a plan for my conversation. I had an exit strategy and everything, and yes, I was aware of the nerve I had. I went to the meeting prepared to say nothing. And the exact opposite happened. I gave about 100 percent of the details. I discussed the tragedies that I had experienced in my life, which I do not make a habit of doing. I described this calling and let him know that I was doing it with reluctance.

After I told him everything I planned not to say, I left and told him I was going to yoga. He made some suggestions about praying in front of the tabernacle and following the calling. With my heart set on going to yoga, I walked to the car but I was being called to run. For the love of God! What didn't my friend God understand about me wanting to go to yoga? Being the obedient servant that I am, I put on a sweatshirt that I had in my yoga bag and I went for a run. As I am running, I was prompted to follow a course through the park behind the church, and then with urgency, specifically to run through a path in the woods that led back to the church. The path was identical to one that had popped up on my computer randomly, as a screen saver, on the day I discovered I was on this path with my editor. This realistic vision was one I had seen earlier. Very Powerful. I ran to my car and I was called to take my journal and get to the church and sit by the tabernacle and write. As I write about all that I had just experienced, I was then told to bring this writing back to Fr. Neutral. With obedience being a lesson that I had earned an A+ in, I did this hoping to land a spot in the AP class. Dying inside, I walked to the rectory and handed him my journal. I have now done everything that I swore to my editor I would not do, all for the love of God!

In reflecting, my reluctance came from knowing that when I put "it" out there "it" becomes real. But the reality was that, aside from the dark parts, this was the coolest thing that had ever happened to me in my entire life. I was becoming aware that this was exactly where I was supposed to be my entire life. I felt whole, pure, and at total peace. My entire life finally made sense. Every millisecond made sense. I had never been so sure of anything. It was the most liberating feeling that I had ever felt. I was not interested in anything that was less than pure. I had no problem admitting it. I sought peace and truth. I wanted nothing more than to continue on this journey.

I want to sprint! Got sneakers?

A SEPARATE LESSON ON SILENCE AND COMMUNICATION

So here I was in a common situation: I reached a breaking point with my husband who had anxious moments. During these moments, I was to become a life raft that was to bring him to safety. Most times, this task could be carried out in a successful manner. However, there were times when the life raft was deflating and had nothing left to give, almost like the tree in the book *The Giving Tree.* (If you haven't read it, read it. It's a children's book. Perhaps I will take my own advice and revisit it.) When the raft needed to abort the mission of saving someone else because it needed to save itself, the struggling swimmer had to become his own swim coach and find his way to safety on his own. If he hadn't mastered the crawl stroke, he would just have to tread water, do the breast stroke, or find a life vest to throw on. The bottom line was that peace would come, but it had to come from within one's own being. We could never totally depend on someone else for our own inner peace and strength. We could look for support, but eventually it had to come from within.

While I was in the moment, I looked to my friend, God, for help and support. And while I neared my breaking point with this anxious moment that I was trying to patiently handle, I suggested going to the chapel with my husband. We were not at peace in the car. He was not understanding this journey and was trying too hard to understand something that, as my brilliant, patient editor pointed out in an earlier chapter, was a mystery. There were moments that we could not understand things, and in those moments, we needed to give it to God. While for some, this task could be easy, for others it is very hard; as hard as moving a mountain. In the chapel, I was looking for my friend God, to advise, console, and give me the words that He always had. I was searching for my team, and what did I get? Silence. I heard a few whispers, "Rest now in me…" and "Silence." So, here I was in my moment of need, and I had to learn to accept silence. OK, I was a bit annoyed with my friend, God, but I had faith and I was respecting the silence. I had to, because I had no choice. What was I to do? Stand on my kneeler in the chapel and yell like a crazy woman and demand a conversation? It didn't work that way. So, silence it was.

On the car ride home from the chapel, I became a preacher as I tried to explain my frustration. Here I was accepting a journey that was uncertain. Clearly, I had accepted it, or you would not be reading this chapter. While I was traveling on an uncertain path, I was being thrown curve balls by my husband that I had to field and throw back. But there comes a point when the curve balls have to stop coming. If I had given it to God, then he must too. We talked about praying, and what he had said in the chapel, and how he had prayed. His prayer was simple: "Trust *it*." He repeated that phrase. So now the constructive criticism came. I explained when you are sitting with your friend, God, have a conversation. Talk to the guy like you would a friend. Ask Him for help. Turn the "trust it" into "here I am, Lord, I do not get any of this, but please help me. Help me give my worry to you. Help me trust this process and journey." I asked him, "Do you get it?" For the love of God, throw me a lifeline! How could I keep explaining something that there was no answer to, something I was following with all my heart with nothing but blind faith? When I started becoming anything but peaceful, I realized that I must get my act together and find peace in silence, which I attempted to do.

When I arrived home, in an attempt to find my peace, I sat and texted my editor and asked, "What lesson am I missing? What do I have to learn so that I am not *forever* in this spot of frustration in being a life raft?" She brought me to silence, my silence that was not respected when my husband wanted to sink the life raft. I gathered the strength and did not allow the sinking of this ship. Next, I saw my student swimmer leaving the house and taking a ride in the car.

Upon arriving home, while I was sleeping, I heard, "Can we talk? I just got back from the chapel where I sat in silence and talked to God the way you told me to." While I was thinking *Amen* and *Alleluia*, I was also prompted to be silent, so I was. When the morning arrived, I was prompted to speak and had the conversation that I didn't have the night before. And here it was, the lesson on silence. Silence has many layers. All need to be respected. There is silence that we meet up against that will cause us unrest because we are looking for communication and do not get it. In these moments we need to respect the silence because, with faith, the words will come in time, and be the ones we need. There is silence that offers us inner peace and strength. In these silent times, we can heal. Finally, there is mutual, peaceful, respected silence, followed by great communication, and when achieved, it is a beautiful *gift*. Who wouldn't want that?

HOW TO SAVE A LIFE

The day started with my new Friday Jesus freak routine of morning prayer. There were two servings: one at 6:00 a.m. for a prayer group sister who worked full time, and a second serving for another bunch at 8:35ish after dropping kids off at school. We met in my not-so-tidy kitchen because that was the reality of life – kitchens were just as messy as life. If my house had to be in perfect order every Friday morning, perhaps we wouldn't pray. So here we were in the kitchen, praying the St. Rita novena. It truly was a beautiful moment. The whole day was to be beautiful. My editor and I planned to spend the day with each other getting my life in order, as this spiritual journey had turned my life upside down. Upside down in the sense of not being able to food shop, make bank deposits for my business, exercise, and hand-in forms for my daughter's middle school registration. This journey had been all consuming and my life had been put on hold.

My wisdom and compassion-filled editor recognized this and threw down a plan for me to get caught up on my life. After prayer we were very productive. We picked up groceries, put them away, and then I was dropped off at the middle school to conduct registration, while Little Miss Editor went to the bank to make a deposit. After all was completed, we were to pray together at the eleven thirty daily Mass, and then organize my writing. Moments before we were to attend Mass, my phone sounded with a text from one of the prayer girls who was in crisis. She was in need of assistance, as she was struggling with anxiety, and felt that she could not be alone. She asked for help to get to the doctor and was too fearful to drive. With a call to the editor to change our plans, and a confirmation from my friend in need that the editor could come, we were off to do God's work and help a friend. Clearly, we were not "needed" at Mass, but we were needed to assist a woman in distress. With a road trip to the doctor, we counseled her in the car until we arrived at the office. The conversation with the doctor led to the realization that she had depressed thoughts coupled with anxiety. This dose of reality resulted in a very tearful prayer group sister whom we embraced with nothing but acceptance and unconditional love. In order not to feel the emotion that we poured out to our sister in need, you would have had to be an emotionless, lifeless rock. With a vow to help our sister, we dropped her home, so that she could rest and process the events of the day.

As we tried, it became more than obvious that we were exactly where we were meant to be, traveling on a path where the destination was unknown but the goal was to help everyone along the way.

Next Stop: Philadelphia.

With peace in my heart, and the goal of handing it out to those in need, I planned a trip to see my sister-in-law, Kerrie, in Philadelphia. With my head ready to explode from information and peace overload, my editor made the arrangements for me to meet Kerrie in Philly. With the ticket purchased, I looked forward to the meeting. I kept in touch with her via email and text. I had noticed that my peace seemed to be reaching her. She started to note it herself. She even mentioned it in a text. My heart felt happy. With a happy heart, I made a chapel run and felt confirmation that Kerrie was in a better place and on a better path.

With the arrival of my "business trip" to Philly came mixed emotions: excitement, awe, joy, and concern that I would have the right words. But I quickly realized that the Holy Spirit would guide me and give me every word that I needed. Deep in my heart, I knew that this trip would be flawless, because I was following God's plan, and how could His plan be less than perfect?

My editor picked me up at the exact moment we planned. We drove to the train station without one ounce of traffic. Next we discussed my husband's most recent anxious moments. I had a calmness about me that I could not explain. Riding in the car seemed like a surreal moment. Was this really happening? Was I really following a plan that was thrown down in the chapel by my angel-faced brother? Was I really meant to save a life with my peace? It seemed as if I was dreaming.

Stepping out of the car and walking to the station made everything real. I could smell the city, feel the heat of the day, and see the arrival and departure boards. Because I was in my peace bubble, I wanted to be sure that I had the correct platform for my trip. Standing next to me was a police officer, and he confirmed that I was to walk up the stairs on the right-hand side. When I arrived, I met a young girl who had never travelled on the train before, and trust me, I was no Amtrak expert, but I assured her that she was in the right place and we chatted. As we spoke, this young nervous girl became calm. When the train rolled in, I got on, looked for a seat, and moments later discovered that I was sitting in front of a priest. He was on the phone with someone, and as he was chatting, I was scribing his every word into my phone, because his words were words that needed to be remembered. He was clearly counseling an anxious individual, and his words were the perfect ones that I could deliver to my husband. So there it was: God was talking via the priest and I was listening. When the priest used the term "sons of bitches," I knew he was my kind of priest!

With a flawless train ride, I arrived in Philly in exactly one hour, and had two hours to spare before lunch. I had a big decision to make: to shop or go to a shrine. As I decided to go to the St. Rita National Shrine with the extra time I had, I sent a text to my editor. Her reply was simple: "With extra time you should check out shrine." Clearly, great minds think alike! I had said the St Rita Novena with the prayer girls. Stepping out of the train station and onto the streets of Philly, there was a taxi waiting to take me to the shrine. After a quick ride I was there. The moment I entered the shrine, I felt a peace that was so extraordinary. I was the only one there. I walked around and prayed in front of every statue: St. Michael, St. Therese Lisieux, St. John the Baptist, St. Augustine, St. Monica...the list goes on. While I prayed in front of St Rita, I wrote out every petition I had in my heart, and placed them in the basket. Walking around in awe, I discovered that I could go to confession and then Mass. I had hit the lotto! During Mass, the homily was so meaningful, that I actually took out my journal and started taking notes. The priest spoke of loving your neighbor. He said, "There is a difference between praying for people to be converted to turn away from sin and witnessing their sin by welcoming sinners to dinner. You do not have to have *dinner* with the *sinner*! For spiritual safety, stay away from sinners. Jesus would not witness prostitution." At that moment it was as if the priest was talking to me. I had been struggling with forgiving and moving through a situation where I had been profoundly hurt. I felt as if I could forgive but I was not interested in "having dinner" with the person who hurt me. And there it was, my answer, clear as day, "You do not have to have dinner with the sinner." Brilliant! After these brilliant words were spoken, I looked at my watch to see that two hours had passed, and I had to make a very brief stop in the gift shop before I left, for time was running out.

In the gift shop, I found a nun and the priest who had given the homily. As I gathered books that I was prompted to purchase, I realized I must hurry. I quickly grabbed some prayer cards and medals of St Rita and

St. Dymphna (patron saint of nervous and mental disease). I walked to the register and the nun asked me if I had come to the shrine for St. Rita's feast day (May 22). I told her that I was in town to see my sister-in-law. She replied, "Are you to be reacquainted with her?" I explained that it had been a long time since I had seen her. She looked at me and said, "Did Rita bring you together?" And although I was in shock, I said, "I didn't think about it, but I guess so." She went on to tell me that Rita had indeed brought us together, and I felt like I had been called to bring Kerrie peace. This nun, who somehow knew my every thought, now told me that she knew that I loved my brother very much. Well, that comment nearly brought me to my knees. So, I looked at her, and told her that I do, and that he was no longer with us. She told me not to worry, because Rita was with me, and my lunch would go well. As I was leaving, she gave me a prayer card. Prior to this I had been feeling my brother's presence. The prayer card said, "Make yourself familiar with the angels, and behold them frequently in spirit; for without being seen, they are present with you" by St. Francis de Sales. Clearly, she was aware of my angel brother's presence. And it was no shock that I had recently been reading the book *Introduction to the Devout Life by Saint Francis de Sales.*

The great thing about this trip to Philly, was that since I had run several half-marathons in this city with my husband in the past, I knew the city well, especially the area where Kerrie was staying. She was actually staying in the hotel where we had stayed in the past for several half-marathon weekends. In addition, my sister worked in Philadelphia, knew the city like the back of her hand, and was just a quick text away. The Kerrie that I met in the lobby of the hotel was a happy, smiling Kerrie, a Kerrie who had joy in her heart. After a big fat embrace, we started walking to the restaurant for lunch. When we sat down, I took out a Pandora box, for I had gotten her an angel charm with my brother's prompting. It was a "one for her, one for me" purchase. The result: two sisters-in-law with matching angel charms. Her eyes lit up upon opening it, and again, when I showed her mine. Clearly, we would be with each other at all times.

The lunch was fabulous! We spoke of life's hurts and joys. We spoke of the expectations that became reality, and the expectations that never led to fullness. We spoke of anxiety and how to deal with it. I shared with her a piece of my heart, when I discussed my husband's anxiety, that had been causing me to become a sinking ship. She listened, advised, and brought me peace. I loved that she brought me peace. The moment she delivered the advice from her own experience, I couldn't wait to throw it out to my husband. At that moment, I loved this journey even more (if that was possible). While together, it even got to the point where we were completing each other's sentences. Our lunch was a true gift from God.

What gifts have saved your life?

MOVING THROUGH DARKNESS

With an upcoming family reunion, we headed to the Catskills. As I sat with my husband and children, looking at the beautiful mountains that surrounded me, I thought of the lessons I had learned this week, and more importantly earlier today. For today, I had encountered the part of this journey I do not enjoy: darkness. While writing this, it occurred to me that I had become the Carrie Bradshaw of spiritual essays. For those who are unaware of this character, she was a writer in a show and movie, Sex in the City. I think my show would be called Spirituality in the Suburbs.

This morning, at Mass, I listened to a homily. It spoke of justice, Jewish law, and loving out of obligation. After the homily, I was left with the following questions… Aren't we to love from the heart? Aren't we to attend Mass because we want to? Aren't we to follow the commandments out of wanting to? Clearly, I was confused. So, I concluded that we are obligated to love our enemies. Well, that didn't sit well with me. With the unrest I found in processing the homily, I drafted an email to the priest who I thought might not be on this path…and SURPRISE. He came up HUGE.

I started the email asking him to explain in great detail what I did not understand. I will do my best to paraphrase a brilliant explanation. In following the "law" (the teachings of the Church, the Commandments) we are to use it as a guide to lead us and give us a path with clear directions… following a road map on a journey. It is the following of the "law" where we learn right from wrong. We have this guide when we cannot act out of love. "Since we are weak and do not always act from virtue, rather we act out of a sense of obligation, it is the thing to do." (his words, it was stated so well I didn't want to mess with it!) Eventually this law leads us to acting out of love.

After digesting these very helpful words, I was so happy to gain a greater understanding of Jewish law, love, and justice. Ah, justice, now there's a word…doing the right thing. While I feel like I pride myself in doing the right thing, at moments, it is so very hard to do. For, at times, it feels like the "Just" stand alone. I have learned the "Just" of this world do not do the popular thing, which is often easier. Acting in a just manner means stepping outside your comfort zone to find the pure hearts of the world. While it is rewarding in the end, the actual moment of standing alone is extraordinarily difficult, but truly are we really ever alone if GOD is our eternal companion? In the dark moments it feels as if we are alone but in reflecting back we are never alone. To give greater understanding of this, I will speak of the darkness that led me to writing this very chapter. In the end, I am thankful for the darkness, because it has brought tremendous light. Without the very darkness I would never have had the neon-lit moments that also followed.

Here we go. With the arrival of Friday, came excitement. I knew that I would be meeting with my prayer girls...the "SISTAhood". It always amazes me what results in simple prayer. Our prayer is not grand... rather it is as simple as the crumbs on my floor in the kitchen. It is simple yet beautiful. It is real... the real deal. Our prayer comes in many forms. It can be a simple rosary that is said, a video that is watched, with a discussion that follows, a novena that we all vow to say, or, at times, we can just attend daily Mass. In addition, it can be in the form of meeting a friend for a walk while discussing and digesting the homilies I have heard, when by myself. And that was what happened one Friday morning. I was up, dressed and excited to speak of justice, Jewish law, and loving out of obligation. As we talked, we walked, and we discussed. With the peace that continued to surround me it was only natural for a wave of darkness to roll in.... a test of my spiritual strength. While on Fifth Ave, as we walked toward church, (a direction we typically did not walk but I felt called to walk that way this particular morning) there it was: temptation and darkness at one specific intersection.

I encountered some "Non-Christian-like Christians" with whom my truthful tongue and "just" nature had led to my demise. For when I had spoken the truth to the queen bee, I was immediately shunned and OUTED.... yup OUT-ed by the church ladies. The queen bee hypocrite turned herself into the "victim", while I, a girl who spoke the truth, became the "attacker." Bottom line is that people do not like the truth, and I had spoken it one morning and then another. While my beliefs were shared among the others, they chose a path where the truth was never spoken to the queen bee.... a path that excluded me and made me the attacker. It was a painful situation, a betrayal in its finest form. But, it was also real life. I learned that the "JUST" of this world stand alone and there aren't many who choose a path where truth, sincerity, and doing the right thing are the exception and not the norm. When this situation initially happened, it brought me to my knees, as if I were kicked in the gut; it made me cry a river and feel sick to my stomach to the point I couldn't eat. I felt as awful as I felt when I lost my two brothers. Yup, as terrible as I felt when I was in the midst of grief. I kept asking myself the question.... "How could *Christian* women allow this to happen?" It wasn't what the other women said; it was what they didn't say. It was the lack of acknowledgement of the pain that was inflicted on another human being. It was the allowing of the queen bee to push someone out of a Christian group. Funny, because I am pretty sure that Jesus would not have treated me this way. Perhaps Jesus Himself would have been treated this way and He would have turned the other cheek. Trying to be more Christ-like, and having time on my side, I had tried to do this, because after all, that was what Jesus would want. I had gone to confession, and spoken to priests about this unfortunate event, that I could not seem to move through. I had even met the queen bee in the chapel in hopes of offering peace to the situation. Perhaps she took it from me, but I never got it back in return. But what I did get back was an ugly, dark feeling while in her company. It was, as if being in her company, compromised my spiritual safety.

At this intersection, I felt like the joy was stolen from my heart and replaced with hate. One of the girls tried to keep the peace as she shouted out to me and tried to engage in conversation. I tried to be gracious but it was so hard, and both she and I knew that this small talk was not mending my broken heart. Facing the betrayal head on brought me to a very dark place. It was like Satan himself knocked me off my peaceful path, and was tempting me to be less than graceful and act in a hateful manner. With my prayer sisTA by my side, I dug deep within me, walked to my Church, and found the Statue of the Blessed Mother. I asked her to take this dark moment and to be with me. We prayed and continued walking. I cried and talked and let it out, and we spoke of justice, injustice, temptation, distraction, and darkness. We prayed and she comforted me. Arriving home, I couldn't shake the wave of darkness. It was as if I was engulfed in a wave of evil and I was caught in a riptide. As I was fighting to be saved, I had to make a decision to go to church or not. I was so sad and filled with hate. As the tears were flowing and with hate in my heart, I sent a text to my editor explaining my plight; she comforted and advised me to get to church. With a face that looked like it had been punched, and tearful eyes, I arrived at daily 8 a.m. Mass late. As I fought back the tears in Mass, I tried so hard to concentrate and ask for God's help.

Still tearful after Mass, I saw my other prayer sisters (sisTAS) and one of them asked if I was ok. I told her to pray for me as I had hurt feelings. Having left to drop off my daughter to summer school, I headed back to church ambulance style with Christian music playing. I needed to be back in Church to say the rosary in hopes of ridding myself of the darkness, that had entered my soul, and had such a hold on it. As I entered Church, I noticed one of the priests that I had spoken to in confession about forgiveness, forgetting, and repentance. He was aware of my struggle. It was the perfect opportunity to chat but, here was the problem, I had NOT ONE WORD. When I needed my words the most they were GONE. So I sat and tried to pray the rosary... and guess what... I could not remember the words for the Our Father, a prayer I say every day. With that, I took out a prayer book and READ the prayer. I said the rosary with the assistance of a cheat sheet. As this priest left, I could barely say hello, but I could look at Mary and beg for help. While praying to Mary, she looked different.... I can't explain it. It was like there was an extra brightness around her. I am not even sure if that was the case because my eyes were flooded with tears. I was so sad that I felt this darkness and that I had a heart that was heavy.

Upon leaving the Church, I saw another one of the priests. It was as if God placed him in my path. Initially, I had no words, but as I was pulling out of the parking lot, I called out to him. I explained my struggle. He listened while I spoke. I tried to make sense of the darkness. Knowing that I had placed this in his hands, I had faith it would turn around. Next, I reached out to my editor and companions on this journey. I was in contact with my editor, as I traveled with my family to the Catskills for a family reunion. I told her every dark thought. I felt so sad as I drove further away from God's house, my safe house. The darkness was so heavy and ugly. I felt as if it were slowly killing me. I begged for prayers from all my companions as I spoke with my husband. True to form, he met this dark moment with compassion, unconditional love, and patience. He was the face of Jesus, the calm in the storm. I knew I would be saved but I had to walk through the storm. That I did, and I came out on the other side.

The greatest thing about darkness is the light that follows. The next day I had to attend a wedding where I would see the silent sinners, the girls who never had my back. In my darkness, I was sure that I would meet them with a sharp hateful tongue or perhaps I would not attend the wedding, but in a belief of being "just" and doing the right thing, I decided to drive home two hours with my husband, to attend the wedding. Everything was perfect...the trip, my dress, my shoes, and most importantly my husband. My husband became "Wedding Chris." Wedding Chris is the guy who is the envy of all. He is the guy who spins his wife on the dance floor as if she is a contestant on Dancing with the Stars. He is the guy who pours out joy and love, and I am the wife that has nothing but grace, joy, and love in return. With the first set of music playing, we were like Fred and Ginger, graceful and loving. It was the real deal, no faking... nothing but pure love poured into us ... a true gift of the Holy Spirit. We became the talk of our table, and the talk of the guests at the wedding. And truly, we were just Wedding Chris and Mary Jo. While we were used to it, others observed us in awe, wanting a piece of it. We raised the bar at our table, as all the couples hit the dance floor. It was something to see, feel, and be a part of. It was the Holy Spirit doing His best work ever and we were the messengers of love. Without the Holy Spirit's presence, this NEVER could have happened because my heart had been filled with hate 24 hours prior. May God bless us and the Holy Spirit's presence... for what happened was like magic.

As I close, I pose this question, when you are met with temptation and darkness, will you attack it with love or hate?

I say love is the answer. How about you?

I HAVE FOUND A
PROM DATE

Early on in this journey, with the peace that had been surrounding me (and continues to), I felt as if I needed spiritual direction. It seemed natural to seek the advice of a priest. Each time I tried to establish contact, I was met with silence. If you remember from previous chapters, I had not been happy with silence because I am very chatty by nature. I had met with two priests on separate occasions and had learned, in time, that they were not the guys for the job. Feeling like a girl who wanted to attend the prom but had no date, my tenacity led me to pursue my longing for spiritual direction. I googled spiritual direction, and to my surprise, I found a program that I could apply to be a part of, close to my home. With excitement and happiness in my heart, I read the application to learn that in order to be a part of the program, I needed to have been under spiritual direction for three years – yup, three years. I thought to myself, "God, you must be kidding me. My patience is running thin!" With this thought, I recalled that part of this journey was learning many lessons, and one of them, was patience. Again, I thought, "For the love of God, haven't I been patient enough?" Here I was ready to serve, I had my running sneakers on and laced, I was at the starting line, and the race would not start.

With all these thoughts swirling around in my head, I reached out to one of my "frat brothers." I asked Father Neutral if he could recommend a spiritual director. He did, and I was back on track with excitement and laced-up sneakers. As I further researched the program, I discovered that the presenters of it, just like me, had combined backgrounds of math and psychology. I am a math teacher and a school psychologist. How dreamy, how heavenly, how perfect. In addition, one of the directors of this program was a graduate of the college I had attended, and where my father had taught. It was as if my dad, straight from heaven, dropped this program in my lap. With hope and anticipation of putting this spiritual direction ball in motion, I emailed the contact. I heard back with a suggested time to meet – three months down the road. This I could accept.

With time marching on, I continued attending daily Mass, praying with my prayer sisters, visiting the chapel, both alone, and with friends. Then one evening I noticed in the bulletin of my "chapel parish" an advertisement for a retreat entitled "The Prodigal Son." I thought to myself, *How perfect! I will have to invite my mom.* God was talking and I was listening. Mentioning it to my mom was as delightful as the sun on a warm, bright day. She was so appreciative and I was so excited. Perhaps this retreat will enlighten both of us. Conducting my research appropriately, I learned that the retreat was to be run by the priest that was the head of the spiritual direction program. While at this glorious retreat, which was not in my hometown parish, we knew not one soul. Who cared? Not us. Upon arriving, in a brief interaction, the woman running the retreat introduced herself, and there was a connection between us, a connection hard to put into words. I noted the feeling and embraced the opening of the retreat.

During the lunch break, I engaged myself in conversation with the priest running the retreat – an extraordinary soul, so extraordinary I felt nothing but peace in his presence. Yes, peace, or should we call it the Holy Spirit? We spoke of spiritual direction, his program, finding a spiritual director, and that I was led to the deacon with whom he works. In addition, I mentioned that I would like to get started before the three-year prerequisite. To my dismay, he advised me to find a spiritual director that was separate from the program. He mentioned that there were spiritual directors at the retreat. Bingo! I was reintroduced to the woman who was running the retreat, the very woman that I felt connected to upon meeting. How lucky was I?

After a conversation and a laugh or two, we agreed to set up a time to meet. I was happy to say, "I have found a prom date!" Time would tell that this interaction was simply that: a prom date – a date and not quite a relationship. In my second meeting, when I was ready to bear my soul, she broke up with me. I was told that my spirituality required more than she could give me.

Feeling like a Jesus freak minus the Jesus, I felt isolated, alone, and abandoned. I took these feelings to the adoration chapel and sobbed, I mean sobbed like I did when my brothers' died. I placed my shattered heart in God's hands knowing in time He would lead me where I was meant to be.

Where is God's call taking you?

THE APPRENTICE

Prior to the breakup with my spiritual director, this journey led me to a second date. This was to occur after a morning encounter with God at daily Mass. With the start to what I felt was going to be a great day, I attended Mass. Knowing that I was going to meet with my spiritual director, I was prayerful about my meeting. With no surprise to me, God spoke through the homily. Very simply, very humbly, the priest asked how many of us had ever been apprentices in our lives. Upon hearing this question, I immediately thought back to my days of student teaching and interning as a school psychologist. Still wiping the sleep from my eyes, I did not have the energy to acknowledge the fact that, yes, indeed, I have been an apprentice in my life. Today, again, I would be an apprentice, learning from my spiritual director.

As the priest went on, he spoke of his days of student teaching and his days of being a deacon (which he coincidently served at our parish many years ago). He spoke of the pastor from my childhood and of all the priests I grew up with – very special. As I write, at this *very* moment, I came back to my chapel thoughts from early in this journey. Charity begins in the home. The homily spoke of my home, my home parish of St. Peter's. Clearly, this is where the charity had started for me. In thinking of this, I realized that I had many teachers and had been an apprentice many times throughout my life.

Wasn't it funny that his "apprenticeship" had been spent with the same leaders I looked up to as a child? During that time on my spiritual journey, my parents were driving the bus. I was just a passenger on the bus of faith and followed the law. These words reminded me that we first learn by following the church law, and eventually, we worship out of our own desire. May God bless my parents for being good examples and encouraging me to cultivate my gift of faith. I had been an apprentice to my parents. On this journey, I had been an apprentice to every priest I had listened to preach. I had seen the difference between worshiping by following the law and worshiping out of desire. Let me say, worshiping out of desire is the way to go! I had been left thirsty and hungry, wanting more. I had excitedly anticipated the words that would be delivered at each Mass. Each homily seemed as though it was written just for me. Every single homily, since the onset of this calling, had touched my heart in a way that, at times, was hard to describe. God had spoken to me in so many ways and one of the most enjoyable had been through being an "apprentice" at daily Mass.

It was with humility that I could see that I had been an apprentice to my husband's everyday actions. His actions were Christ-like, in his every thought, word, and deed. He was the face of Jesus on this journey with me and he was finally seeing that in himself. I have learned to be more Christ-like from him. I may add that it was not so easy living with the face of Jesus, but, so very rewarding! It was a true gift.

I was now an apprentice to my spiritual director, yes, my spiritual director. Early on, I never thought I would be able to say I had a spiritual director. And today, another dose of humility was swallowed as I was challenged to re-address my thoughts about the people who had hurt me most in life. I was asked, "If we are all children of God, how can you not see everyone as God's child?" Now that was a side I wasn't seeing! "How is God talking to me in this situation?" Yeah, be careful what you wish for. This spiritual direction was going to require some work. Work that I was so happy to do.

Finally, reflecting on the earlier chapters and my Easter Sunday vision of a wellness center, I envisioned a brick building that appeared to be attached to education. Well, the vision became a reality about a month ago when I was being interviewed for a graduate school program. As I drove with my husband onto the campus of Seton Hall, there it was, the Easter Sunday vision, a brick building at a university that was associated with a Catholic Center for Family Spirituality, and a graduate program that was dreamy, a program so dreamy, that my husband and I would attend together.

So here it is, the story of a girl, my journey, and my calling. A calling that was being followed with every morsel of my being, a call that had brought me to my initial vision, a call that had humbled me, inspired me, and opened my eyes to a world of opportunity to serve and walk the walk. This call would help me go from apprentice to teacher. How lucky was I?

It's been an incredible ride. What will the journey from apprentice to teacher bring? I guess you will have to stay tuned. Are you an apprentice?

NEWARK AIRPORT

Prior to leaving for a trip to Ohio, I attended Mass; the homily theme: Love. In deepening our love relationships, sometimes we must let go.

Was this real? I have put my life on hold to follow a call. I was "letting go" of my old life to embrace my new soul. The old life was much easier, much!

As I sat in the airport, I found myself without hesitation, praying to the Blessed Mother for an adolescent autistic boy, who was becoming disruptive. While I understood he was trapped in his own mind and body, others did not. As the onlookers appeared to become unnerved, and the mother looked so fearful of a potential outburst, I prayed. Within moments the boy was calm and settled, sitting next to his dad. The onlookers resumed their activities. Amen.

What would this pilgrimage bring? What was my purpose? Why was I being called? I had no doubt that all these questions would be answered – not one doubt. So buckle up, because this journey was gaining momentum, that was as strong as God's love for us.

How did I end up in an airport heading to Ohio? About one week ago, I felt a call – yes, a call, a call to go to the chapel, my new hangout. With the call, came the prompting to text my editor to join me. With texts back and forth, I was unsure if she could make it. After waiting for a response, I decided to leave, and if she was meant to be with me, it would happen. As it was intended to be, I received her text as I was getting on the highway. "Did you go?" With that, I called her and said that I was in the car and would be right there. Ambulance style, I turned around and headed back to get my editor and lifeline – yes, lifeline for this crazy journey. Never ever would it have gotten to where it was without her patience and wisdom in the managing of my thoughts. She was a thought manager – full job description to follow later.

When we arrived at the chapel, what we found waiting there was an invitation to go see a visionary who had visions of Jesus, the Blessed Mother, and many saints. I received the invite from my sister at home, only to throw it out, because how was a mother of three children going to drop her life the second week of school, to make a "pilgrimage" to a sacred ground in Ohio. Really? Think about it. It was just crazy. My Jesus freak sister was going and she had attended many. I'm talking countless times and I was very familiar with the "pilgrimage", actually more familiar than I would have liked to admit.

In my heart I felt that her prayers and pilgrimages over the years had brought miracles to my family. My other non-Jesus freak sister had been diagnosed with stage IV breast cancer twelve years ago. She was a survivor. My daughter who suffered from infantile spasms, a severe disorder causing frequent hospitalizations, had her last seizure after my sister prayed, blessed her with holy "pilgrim" water, and touched a hat to her head that had touched the very spot where Mary had appeared to the visionary. So, here I was with an invitation I had already thrown out, coming right back to me boomerang-style.

With brief words exchanged about the invite, we entered the chapel. In the presence of the Lord, I cleared my mind and sat silently. I waited, and like a sudden rain shower, I was flooded with thoughts that I journaled:

> You were called to be here
> You are called to go to Ohio
> You can make it happen
> Never say never.

With a recap call to my sister upon getting home, she explained that what I found in the chapel was a *personal* invitation from the *Blessed Mother*. I stated, "Your group has infiltrated *my* chapel!"

Great. No pressure. How would I RSVP "no" to an invitation like that? I was becoming aggravated and said things like "I can't do this. I have three kids…blah, blah, blah…" My sister responded, "Don't yell at me. This time I did not invite you. *Mary* did!"

For the love of God, this was too much. She explained that I should pray a lot about it, and if it's meant to be, it will all work out. After a week of prayer and amazing insight and wisdom even from my children, as simple as my eldest daughter's quote, "Mom, this is an answer to your prayer. Don't you get it? You prayed to become closer to your sister. This is how your prayer is being answered," and my younger daughter, on my concern over leaving them, said, "Mom, we'll be fine. If you are happy, we are happy. We love you. Don't worry." How could I not go?

What would you do?

MARANATHA SPRING AND SHRINE, ELYRIA, OHIO

What will this trip bring? What is my purpose? Why am I being called?

At this moment, for this chapter, I can only answer the first question. I am sure in time I will be able to answer the others. The most important gift received was the gift of sisterly love. If this was the only gift I gained, then I'd be a winner, but there were many more. Hence, I felt like a champion. My sister had been attending pilgrimages to Maranatha Spring and Shrine for ten years. Over the years, I had imagined how great her experiences must have been, but to experience the moments and to walk the walk myself was very powerful.

For starters, you must understand how different I am from my sister. As I mentioned earlier, we are complete opposites. She is the oldest of the six children in my family. I am the youngest. Her personal style is one of structure at all times. I, on the other hand, am as structured as Jell-O. I live in the moment, at all times, and take life as it comes, case in point: my going on this trip. My sister has dark brown hair and brown eyes. I am blonde with blue eyes. I am athletic and run marathons, while she is the best spectator. We have always been complete opposites. Simply stated, this trip brought to light a common thread: our deep faith, and, for that, I was thankful.

Now with all I have just said contrasting my sister and myself, allow yourself further visualization. Anytime we were together she would say I was like a celebrity, because inevitably I would see someone I knew, my cell phone would sound, and/or my name would be called. She loved to remind me of my extrovert personality. On the contrary, she is an introvert. At times I had thought she was a secret agent for the FBI. I even wondered if all of her "pilgrimages" were actually FBI business trips, because she makes four pilgrimages a year. Honestly, it really was something. Well, buckle up, because on this very pilgrimage there would be a role reversal.

Upon arriving, my sister introduced me as if I were a celebrity. In turn, the pilgrims embraced my "celebrity status." It was quite funny. I then faded into the background, as I took in the whole scene, and this was what I noticed: my sister was like head pilgrim. They all flocked to her. This flocking transformed her into an extrovert – it was amazing. She stepped out of her introversion, all for the love of God! Meanwhile, I assumed the more introverted role as I observed the pilgrims. While doing this, I had moments to chat with Angela's peeps. The love they had for her was so evident, as was the profound respect. While they were so very fond of her, I also saw that they recognized her strong presence, and the manner that they approached her was with compassion. It was a gift for me to observe.

But the greater gift was being a part of the praise and worship service. I am not quite sure I can put this into words. I will do my best. Angela had alluded to the fact that we would be singing and dancing. My "live in the moment" personality thought "whatevs…" for I knew that I'd just roll with it. Well, my friends, nothing, nothing, could have prepared me for seeing my "secret agent" sister in action – I mean nothing! She was clapping and singing like I had never seen. She was like a Jesus freak rock star. I was in such shock that I truly thought I might wet my pants. No worries, I remained dry. While being present in the moment, and not all at the same time, I had the ability to make a realization that her enthusiasm and non-secret agent behavior, was a direct result of God's love for her, and hers for Him. She was praising God in song and dance. At this moment, I realized I had better brush up on my Christian rock dance moves!

Who knew that my friend, God, was such a fan of this Christian rock-style worship and healing. Ah yes, the healing. I had failed to mention this was a praise and worship healing gathering. As I was trying to adjust to this change in music genres from my good old-fashioned Bruce Springsteen and transition to Christian rock, I observed the healing aspect. I became aware of the gifts of the Holy Spirit, and just as I had been bestowed with the gift of words, the woman leading the service was bestowed with the gift of healing. With the praising, singing, and dancing came a leader who was leading us in prayer celebrity-style. To get the proper visual, picture a woman in a short-sleeved shirt, shorts, and flip-flops working up a sweat because truly she was on fire with the Holy Spirit's presence. While we were praising God, she spoke of feelings that she was taking on from others. As she "felt" a particular ailment, she called it to our attention. If the ailment was something that was one of ours, or belonged to someone we were personally praying for, we owned it – dance style with an "Amen" and "Praise God." Once owned, she confirmed that healing will take place.

Now, like you perhaps, I was thinking, "You must be kidding me!" Even with testimonials from other pilgrims, I still felt I had to see this for myself. So I started praying for my sister, my friends, and any healing intentions that came to me. I was watching other pilgrims "own" ailments until I found myself, like a Jesus-loving dancing queen, praising God and high-fiving other women when we prayed for relationships, especially for single women to meet holy men. I thought Angela and I were going to fall down. Well, "Amen" and "Praise God," I would dance on the table to make this "healing" a reality for her. As the service continued, I owned healings for very close friends. I will assure you there will be testimonials when these healings occur.

Returning to the question "What will this trip bring?" I think it is rather obvious that, with the awareness of God's love for us and ours for Him, extraordinary things can occur. It is clearer than ever, that with His love, *anything* is possible.

What needs to become possible for you?

SETON HALL UNIVERSITY

Waking up one morning, I had an excitement within me – an excitement that you might feel on the first day of school. I took this childlike feeling of joy, to the campus of Seton Hall University, where I was currently attending graduate school. I was on my way to a meeting with my professor to discuss my class selection for next semester. Parking on the campus could be challenging, but not for me on this beautiful crisp and sunny fall morning. As I walked to the meeting, I thought, "What am I doing here? I am taking classes that I cannot afford. I am running on a treadmill to nowhere. I am writing a book that may never be published. I am working very hard and making sacrifices… for what?"

With these thoughts in my head, I walked into the seminary. I took in my surroundings. I paused a moment to listen to my heart. I was so happy, as happy as a girl on her wedding day. I processed the moment and walked into my meeting for advisement. I was brief in my comments about my current classes. The lack of words was not consistent with my chatty personality. I was holding back. In my life I had learned that there was always a vision and then there existed the reality. While sometimes they matched, other times they did not. When vision and reality did not become one, I had learned acceptance. I had accepted that my first two classes were not as dreamy as I had envisioned them. I enjoyed learning and being in this beautiful environment. I was so very thankful for all the wonderful people I had met. I took notes until my arthritic wrist throbbed. I accepted the beauty of a group dynamic and I learned from it. I had also learned that I would move forward holding onto the hope that my next class would be the merging of my vision and reality.

After my meeting, with so many thoughts floating around in my head, I sat and then texted my dear friend, the editor, with tears in my eyes. I had come to thoughts that this whole experience was a joke, the biggest tease ever. I sat on a bench and could see, hear, taste, touch, and smell the academic environment. I breathed it in; all while I had this sinking feeling it would most likely be a reality only for a short period of time. I was waiting for the pennies from heaven to finance this degree, and it hadn't rained a drop. I was in a drought, but I accepted the dry conditions because I had no choice. But what I did have was great faith. I had faith that God would provide because He always did.

I took my penniless faith to the most magnificent chapel on the campus of Seton Hall University. As I opened the door, I was nearly knocked down by a gusty wind of peace. I felt as if I was being hugged by peace itself. As I looked forward, to my surprise, I saw that the Blessed Sacrament was exposed. My heart was so very happy. I prayed. I sat in silence and listened to the dialogue that entered my mind. A dialogue I didn't plan or ask for – words, meaningful words that were now mine, sacred words that I treasured, and tucked into my heart. I sat and I felt the presence of the loved ones in my life who had become my own personal angels. I traveled with an army of them. As I took in the beauty of the moment, I realized the significance of the day. Today, November 2nd, was the feast of All Souls' Day. After praying the rosary, I was off to get a student ID card.

In the ID card room, I was my chatty self. I was light-hearted and witty with the worker and he responded in kind. Within moments there was a peaceful air to the room. Of course, he found great humor and commented when he learned I was a theology graduate student. It was like I said a dirty word. I rolled with every joke, and since I grew up with three older brothers, I gave it right back to him. In his dishing it out, he asked, "So are you going to be a saint?" I giggled because yesterday had in fact been All Saints' Day, and every last saint that I had studied for my mid-term exam, was floating around in my head. In jest, I said to him, "You just never know, but you may want to note my name!" As I said this, I was on fire. I was my peaceful, floating-on-air self, and this worker was the recipient of my peace delivery.

After this exchange, I floated back to the chapel for noon Mass. To my surprise, I served as a Eucharistic minister with a trinity of priests – yup, the priests and me. I was a bit awestruck on the altar. That was an understatement. I cannot put the feeling into words. It was an ineffable moment. While serving the Blood of Christ, I was blessed to hand the chalice to a friend of mine... what a special moment.

With the close of Mass, I reflected on the homily, which linked two very meaningful days in the church: All Saints' Day and All Souls' Day. The homily was so very beautiful, so very special. For me, it was extraordinary. In reflecting back on the entire day, I realized that I now could answer the very question I posed earlier, "What am I doing here?" I was at Seton Hall University for every extraordinary moment I could breathe in.

If we are called to model our lives after the saints and this was one way I could do that, than why wouldn't I? Would you?

WHAT IS HOME?

Today, I had the opportunity to attend a retreat in my parish. I had been attending all week and it had been quite wonderful. The morning started with Mass and then we met for Bible study afterward. We had been praying the Psalms – beautiful. As stated earlier, typically I was chatty by nature. In fact in my youth while attending Catholic elementary school, I was often known to land a spot in the hallway for "sharing" my gift of gab with classmates. During these times, I would pray that my mother, a teacher in the school, would not be walking down the hallway. Fortunately, she never discovered me. At a young age, I would whisper in a small voice, "Thanks, God." What I had found odd about my participation in this retreat was my silence…yes, my silence. I was learning to love silence. It is in silent moments that we hear the sound of God's voice. But how many of us truly stop to listen?

I had been listening so much that I felt, if I were to look in the mirror, I might find that my ears had turned into those of an elephant. But, better to have elephant ears than an elephant's caboose! Today, as I listened, I heard the following:

> As Christians we have the *golden gift of faith*...
> We use it until the finish line...It is a full-time
> job being a Christian with the golden gift. The
> use of one golden gift leads to many others. We
> use the golden gift of faith to benefit others.

These were just some of the words that touched my heart during the homily. Today's words make me reflect on yesterday's words.

> Praying scripture yields grace. Grace leads to
> changed behavior. God is present in the *Word*
> as well as in the *Eucharist*. Grace just comes.
> You don't order it. It just comes.

Think about that. "Grace just comes. You don't order it, and it just comes." For me, this was so very true of my spiritual journey. The many things that I had been experiencing in prayer had been a part of God's grace – how sacred. I could never ever order it. How did one order feeling a fatherly presence sitting next to you? How could you order a visit from a loved one who resided in the eternal resting place? How did one order a conversation that comes to mind, out of nowhere, when praying in an adoration chapel? These graces could not be ordered. If they could, I would have put together some menu. It might read:

Today's Specials

Monday: Chapel visits that include an invisible hug upon entering. A hug so powerful you may buckle at the knees.

Tuesday: An overwhelming feeling of your father and brothers' presence, all who are angels. Presence includes words and meaningful phrases for you and family members.

Wednesday: Prayers answered with a sign that was asked for, a sign in the form of a mark that resembles a cross and rests in the palm of your hand.

Thursday: A homily that seemed to be a personal conversation with God. A homily that delivered every word that was meant for your ears.

Friday: Silence. Peaceful silence that delivers a peace that makes you feel as if you were walking on air.

Saturday: A delivery of words to be written that could change someone's life. Enough words for a non-writer to write a book.

Sunday: An urge to call a friend in need to discover your phone call made a difference.

My menu would be very long, for the examples were endless. In my silence, I reflected on the *golden gift of faith* and my own talents. Where were they to lead me? At this moment, they led me *home*. But, what was home? I think that home is where we find Divine Love. On our spiritual journey, it is our hope that Divine Love resides in our hearts. We make a home for our Lord to reside in our hearts. Hence, God dwells in the core of our being. I am not sure about you, but for me, if God is alive in my heart, I am forever changed. I am pretty certain that this is not going to be a humble abode. While I am humbled to have God live in my heart, His dwelling place should be quite spectacular. It seems fitting for Him to build a home that He sees fit. During these moments of construction, we become powerless, but in a good way, as we let Him construct His home in our heart.

If we really thought about this idea of God living within us, we would realize that we no longer drive the bus. We willingly hand the keys over and don't even ask where we are going. Because with God in the driver's seat the possibilities are endless! Every possibility leads you to how to use your golden gift of faith.

This brings me to an expression often heard from my dad, "Charity begins in the home." I had heard it so many times growing up. As a child, I remembered thinking that when we were so busy helping others, we also needed to remember that charity begins in our immediate home, our home of a family of eight. As an adult, I realized that in order for charity to begin in the physical structure of my home, it must first begin in my heart. God must live in our hearts before charity can come to the home of our immediate families and then eventually to our *every Christian action.*

Home... home brought me to the funeral Mass I attended today for a friend's mother who lived her life how I have described. Her home now would be one where she lived with the Lord, her husband, and her son in the eternal home of God. This home was a home that welcomed all, a home where all were fed, a home where as paraphrased in Psalm 36:

> They feast on the abundance of YOUR house, and YOU give them drink from the river of YOUR delights. For with You is the fountain of life: in YOUR LIGHT, WE SEE LIGHT.

Don't you want to live in this home?

JESUS IS A DIRTY WORD

Here I was on this journey. I hadn't a clue where I was headed. I had surrendered to God's Will as I allowed Him to drive the bus. I had met so many extraordinary people on the way. My bus was packed with cheerleaders, those with faith, those without faith, those who were looking for faith, and those who were just silent observers. I loved my bus and all that it had to offer.

This Advent season my bus had been making many stops along the way as I prepared for the birth of baby Jesus. I was "Merry Christmasing" every soul because, like a child with the excitement for the anticipation of Christmas morning, I couldn't contain my feelings. It was so rewarding to see the smiles on the faces of total strangers. It was as if everyone wanted to say it, but everyone also wanted to be politically correct. So I asked myself, "What is so politically incorrect about saying Merry Christmas?" Oops, I said *Christ*. It's not like I had said, "Praise God, transform your soul, love God and your neighbor," but, I had made a subtle reference to Him, with the mere mention of Christ. Now here's the deal from a purely historical perspective. He was a man who walked on this earth. He had some pretty cool friends and did some pretty cool things. Why not celebrate His birthday with a cheerful "Merry *Christ*mas?" We celebrate former presidents' birthdays. We have sales in every store to commemorate them. This tells me that society values the monetary gain associated with these holidays, but not really the meaning behind them. Yet for Presidents' Day, we see pictures of Abe Lincoln and George Washington. Why not display a picture of Jesus for Christmas? He was a part of history.

I took it upon myself to be a bit more vocal about the birth of Jesus in the post office. When I went to buy stamps, I was asked, "Would you like the religious ones?" Not expecting an answer with such fervor, the woman was pleasantly surprised when I responded, "Of course! It is baby Jesus' birthday!" A smile came to this woman that could have lit the darkest path. She was beaming with pride. She looked at me, and went on to say, that it made her so happy that someone was actually acknowledging the reason for the season. We chatted about our faith, about being Christians, and the churches to which we belonged. She was grateful that someone used the name *Jesus*! As I left, I heard, "Miss?" I turned around and she said, "Thanks. That was so special – you are so special." With that I felt like skipping to my car. I think I actually did, and I took my Jesus-loving self onto my next pit stop.

Arriving at Bed Bath & Beyond, I realized that I did not have the coupon for a rather pricey item. In an attempt to get one, I asked several sales associates. While they could not give me one, they advised me to buy the product and to come back with the receipt, and they would gladly issue me a credit. In my head, I thought to myself, "I am traveling today with the Holy Spirit and clearly you are unaware." I felt confident I would have a coupon at the time of the purchase. Feeling badly, my daughter said, "Mom, that's not fair. Why won't he give you the coupon? Now you have to come back?" I told her not to worry and that I had a feeling that we would find one by the time we had to check out. While approaching the line, I saw this lovely couple who could have been my parents. I also saw a woman with a not-so-friendly look on her face. I chose the line with the warm, loving, adorable couple who, by just looking at them, you could tell they were filled with joy.

When my turn arrived and I asked the young college student cashier if there was any way to get a coupon, he explained that it was the store policy that they were not allowed to give them to customers. I accepted his response graciously and he looked relieved. He went on to elaborate that he hated confrontation and was so happy that I had accepted his answer. With that, the lovely couple who were walking toward the exit came back, and said, "Would you like one of our coupons?" I graciously accepted and wished them a "Merry Christmas!" With that a member of my church came up to me and wished me a Merry Christmas, and spoke of us serving as Eucharistic ministers at the Christmas Mass, all while the young cashier listened. He now could not help himself from saying, "Obviously, you are Christian. Me too. What church do you go to? It sounds like a great parish." I spoke of my parish, my faith, and being Roman Catholic. He expressed his belief in Jesus and said, "To me it doesn't matter what formal religion you are. We are all the same…Christians. *We* believe in Christ." Well, how about that?

As I walked back to my car, I thought of a homily that I had recently heard during a retreat. The priest had spoken about having been down south and ordering breakfast. When his meal arrived, he noticed grits on his plate. He kindly told the waitress that he didn't order grits. Her response was simple, "Sir, around here, you don't order grits. You just get them!" He made an analogy to *grace*. You could not order God's grace. You just get it. So, here again, I was the recipient of God's grace, as I was traveling through the Advent season, preparing for the birth of baby Jesus, our Savior.

This entire Advent season had been filled with more grace-filled moments than I could count. As I continued to travel on this journey and I understood that grace was all a part of growing in holiness, I gave thanks for these moments. When they arrived, I enjoyed every millisecond, because I knew that they could not be ordered. Just like today, I couldn't have ordered these words, that I was writing on December 19, while I was supposed to be studying for an exam on the history of Christianity. The words had arrived as I was standing in my kitchen. I took a deep breath, hit pause, and went joyfully to the computer to write. I hadn't had a word delivery in a while. I was curious but patient. I had known they would come when the bus driver knew I was ready. So today, God's grace was sprinkled in the form of words – lucky me!

Today's lesson was on grace. I had a sneaking suspicion that the next lesson would be one on church history. Don't get nervous. It will be my usual Jesus freak style, light breezy, but informative. Perhaps, there will be a joke or two, for God knows I love humor.

I can't wait for the next word delivery.

How about you? And in conclusion, I must ask, "Got grace?"

THE SPIRITUAL MICROSCOPE

Who am I? Where was I? How did I get here?

Early in this journey, that was an easy question to answer. I was a simple girl with simple spirituality. I believed in the golden rule. I treated all in the manner I wanted to be treated. I was free-spirited, and I took the day as it came. I prayed, I believed in God, I was aware of His ever presence in my life. I went to Mass. When I got there, I got there, but when I did get there, I always felt a peace that was hard to explain. I assumed everyone felt that peace. Because for me, in my entire life, the feeling of peace was synonymous with attending Mass. Even as an eighth grader attending Mass with my brother, as my mom sang in the choir, and we would poke fun, singing and laughing, I still found peace. In looking back, there weren't many times when I didn't feel peace. Even while mourning the loss of my brothers and feeling anger toward God, I would go to Mass and feel peace.

Attending Mass was never a chore. In my twenties it wasn't a chore, but it wasn't a priority either. As I said, I attended when I felt like it, when I needed nourishment. I attended when it fit into my schedule, all along justifying not attending by proclaiming my life of being a good person. Some days at college, I found myself in daily Mass, just because. I couldn't explain it, but I had to be there, so I went. Sure enough, God talked to me during those moments and I always listened. Even during the times I attended Mass when it fit in my schedule, God was with me, and He gently reminded me of the path I was on. How kind of Him.

When I realized that it wasn't enough to just attend when I felt like it, I found the time to attend each week. I remembered thinking not attending was like having a best friend that you never made time to visit. Of course, peace was always waiting for me upon entering the church. The peace kept growing and growing. I would ignore it, or perhaps I didn't ignore it, but I just didn't know what to do. There would be a call. I would let it go to voicemail, but the call kept coming; the peace kept coming. Now the peace was here to stay and I was responding to the call.

I responded by attending daily Mass, attending graduate school to study theology, forgiving hurts, accepting things that couldn't be changed, and chatting with wisdom-filled priests about growing in holiness. I responded by praying the rosary, when I felt like that was what I should be doing, praying in an adoration chapel after work, which could be ten at night. In responding, I realized that God was patient as He waits for each of us to respond to His invitation. It's up to us to accept the invitation.

I was in a place where I had to discern what's next. How was I to use my God-given talents? I thought I had been doing that by teaching. It was becoming clear that it was time to change it up and I was happy to do that, as I handed my heart to God, and let Him guide the way. I accepted that I did not drive the bus. It was very liberating. It allowed me to kick back, put my feet up, and let Him guide the journey – pretty cool. Like anything else, acceptance was key to this journey. In answering, "Where was I?" I have to say that I was exactly where God intended me to be. Sometimes we just must be. It's simple and difficult at the same time. I waited, with joy, to see where this journey would take me. I had gotten to this place through prayer, patience, and surrendering to God's Will. In doing so, I had allowed a flashlight to be illuminated on my soul. I had to take a look inside myself and examine each microscopic detail. I had tried my best to accept the good with the bad. In doing so, I had no choice but to rely on God and His plan. Being under the microscope was not easy but very rewarding.

Are you ready to be probed?

SEA OF JOY

"The soul of one who loves God always swims in joy, always keeps holiday, and is always in a mood for singing." Take a moment to reflect on this quote written by St. John of the Cross.

Swimming in joy, always keeping holiday, and always being in a mood for singing, sounds dreamy. In surrendering to God's Will, in letting Him drive the bus, it is possible to swim in a sea of joy. In learning acceptance and forgiveness, I am swimming in a sea of joy.

St. John of the Cross is known for his poem, "Dark Night of the Soul," which speaks of a spiritual crisis on a journey toward a union with God. During darkness of night, we may not feel the presence of the Lord, but we realize that in darkness there is always light. Without a dark moment, we would never be able to experience the bright, shining light on the other side. It was in these moments that I had learned to rely on God, to surrender to His Will.

In surrendering, I had learned acceptance and forgiveness. When I reflected back on situations in which

I had my feelings hurt, and trust me, I mean really hurt, I cringed. I could actually physically feel my anger. My anger was real. It was human. It was normal, but it felt like a poison in my body that caused me to stray from a path, a peaceful, loving path. I tried so hard to resolve the anger. I felt as if I had placed it in God's hands asking Him to take it. I felt as if I was forgiving the hurt and was making an effort to find peace in my heart, but I could not understand why I kept feeling the pain, frustration, anger, and judgment. It was terrible.

In a final attempt to put it all behind me, I made an appointment to speak with one of the priests, good old Father Neutral. As I listened to myself talk, I realized that my idea of forgiving had been with expectations. Expectations that included an acknowledgment of the pain, repentance from the person that had hurt me and an "I'm sorry." As I sat and talked and listened, I started to understand that forgiveness was forgiveness period. Period, end of story. That was all it was, just plain forgiveness. It didn't come with a side of comforting French fries in the form of an acknowledgment, or an "I'm sorry" with a sprinkle of repentance. When we truly forgive, it is simple, yet not, we just forgive. When we simply forgive, we are free, free from the feelings we hold onto that become a poison inside of us. This forgiveness gig was not easy. This had been a long haul for me. It required much time, prayer, patience, and God's grace. If you allow yourself to just "let it go," this equation of time, plus prayer, plus patience, plus God's grace will yield an outcome that exceeds your greatest expectations: total acceptance and forgiveness. It is so liberating.

So now I feel free! I am free of the poison that had caused my writing to include words of darkness, where the anger just jumped off the page. I am free to replace the anger with more peace. I am free to love the way God loves us. I am free to swim in a sea of joy and surrender, as the current takes me to whatever place I am meant to be.

Swimming in a sea of joy is dreamy. Would you like to take a dip?

THE WELLNESS CENTER

About a year ago, I started documenting this journey. It started in my church, my home, God's house, while serving on a pre-Cana team. I had had an overwhelming feeling of the Holy Spirit's presence. I had called it "energy." Let's clear this up. There was *no* energy in the world that could have made me feel the way I felt. There was one and only one Being that brought a peace like this that was indescribable... *The Holy Spirit*. Peace is a gift of the Holy Spirit. We could all receive this beautiful gift, but must be open to it.

> Ask and it will be given to you; seek and you will find; knock and the door will be opened to you. For everyone who asks, receives; and the one who seeks, finds; and to the one who knocks, the door will be opened.
>
> Matthew 7:7–8

How true is this? Straight from the Bible. Look nowhere else. Let the Bible be your compass and that was what I had done. With the Holy Spirit's presence, I asked, "What is Your Will, Lord?" I asked for guidance and help and then this most recent part of my journey started. In my seeking, I had had a vision of a spiritual wellness center. I am still praying about that vision a year later. Perhaps, I am the wellness center. Perhaps, one day there will be a physical structure as well. Perhaps, we are all called to be wellness centers to others, and to treat every single encounter, as if we are encountering God Himself.

I cannot speak for you, but, if I am encountering God, I certainly will act in a manner that embraces the essence of who He is. God is *love*.

How about you? All you have to do is ask, seek, and knock. I have loved knocking on God's door. How about you?

AUTHOR'S NOTE

The end but really the beginning…

It seems fitting, to end with the talk written to the pre-Cana team, one year after the Holy Spirit's presence came into my life, and swept me off my feet. This talk was actually written as an assignment for graduate school. (Yup, I cheated. I offered for my husband and me to give this talk. I knew I had already written it for school!)

Marriage as a Sacrament

In preparing this talk I couldn't help but reflect on the Beatles' song "All You Need Is Love." While they sing of love, love, love, and tell us that's all you need, I thought about married life and wondered, "Is that really true?" I am hoping that I can reflect on married life, love, and marriage as a sacrament. Perhaps, in doing so, we can explore an equation that will yield a successful marriage in the eyes of God.

Several years ago, when my husband and I were asked to be on the pre-Cana team, with an eye roll and resistance, we said yes as if we were being held up at gunpoint. With three young children ages four, seven, and ten, it was not an easy task. In addition to our parental responsibilities, my husband is a high school baseball coach, and pre-Cana was during the baseball season. Having such a demanding schedule made the task seem challenging. But when you are being held up, you have no choice but to say yes.

Serving that year was fun. We sat, we chatted with the couples, and we reflected about our own marriage. I began to realize, in giving to others, we were receiving. Having "done our time," we thought we could check it off the list, until the following year, when the email asked us to reserve time and serve again. I thought to myself, "Are they kidding me?" The kids were a year older, they were involved in activities, my husband was coaching, my in-laws were moving from their home of forty years, and life seemed over-the-top busy. After chatting with my faith-filled mother, I felt as if I was given approval to say no. With my mom's calming words, I was able to formulate my resignation email. When I hit Send, I thought, "Amen. I am D-O-N-E, done." Not having to serve, I felt relieved. Little did I know my resignation was not 100 percent accepted, when I received an invitation the following year to serve. As I mentioned it to my husband, he said to me, "I think we should do it this year. I can't explain, but I think we should be there." With the green light from him, I responded to the email, saying that we were happy to serve.

With arrangements for our children in place, we arrived and greeted the newly engaged couples. We sat, we chatted, we bonded. During one of the breaks, I looked at my husband, Chris, and asked what he thought about serving. He looked at me and responded by saying, "I think I am getting more out of this than I am giving." I simply agreed, as I sat back and listened to the talk on marriage as a sacrament. Listening to the talk, I started thinking to myself, "Have I ever really stopped to think of my marriage as a sacrament?" Growing up in a Catholic home, where a daily dose of faith was as routine as breathing, I think I took this idea for granted. And, while I am a bit embarrassed to admit that, it is in realizing it, that I am able to take a step outside of my marriage, and see that I have been living the sacrament, but not "labeling" it as that.

So what does it mean to live a "sacramental marriage"? What makes our Catholic Christian marriage different? In order to think about this, I think it is best that we consider the meaning of sacrament. Sacrament is defined as a sign and instrument of grace. Sacraments are liturgical rites instituted by Jesus Christ, as channels of salvation for the world.

It is a sign of God's grace. I never really took a moment to think about this. In my marriage, God's grace is with me all the time. As much as the Beatles sing about love, love, love, we need a little bit more than love to have a successful marriage. God's grace is a key ingredient. In reflecting on my own marriage, there were times when I would be on the Beatles peace train singing about my L-O-V-E for my husband and how dreamy life is, but there have been times when I have wanted to jump on an express train out of town! In both situations, I was surrounded by God's grace and never took the time to see it. God's grace is what kept me in the train station, and prevented me from getting on the express train out of town. In those moments, when I was feeling less than love, perhaps anger, or frustration, God's grace led me to prayer. God's grace led me right into my home of St. Peter's, where I begged God to help me have patience in my marriage, have kind words, have the ability to be the face of Jesus to my husband when I might not want to be. In return, I can say that in dark moments, my husband has always been the face of Jesus to me. It is quite annoying because, for him, it seems effortless.

God's grace has brought us to an adoration chapel in both happy and sad times. We have prayed together when we have felt like we wanted to rip the hair out of each other's heads. We have prayed together after having a peaceful dinner around the corner from the chapel. Stopping at the chapel after dinner was like having a second helping of dessert.

In taking a step outside of myself and looking in, I realize marriage is the best example of the trinity. When God is present in your marriage, it is no longer about you and your spouse. It is about what God's Will is for you and your spouse. Your marriage becomes a selfless act. It becomes about you giving of yourself entirely to another. It is about seeing the face of Jesus in each other at all times. It is realizing that marriage is a lifelong commitment. It is realizing that during dark times, God is with you, and you are to turn to Him for support and guidance. We do not jump on the express train out of town, because in doing that, we are walking away from God and His grace. I don't know about you, but I am not interested in doing that. In seeing marriage as a sacrament, we realize that God is the glue that keeps us together during every moment.

In reflecting, about sacraments being liturgical rites instituted by Jesus Christ, as channels of salvation to the world, I think about how blessed we are to have the gift of a Christian marriage. Marriage is a liturgical rite. We celebrate this sacrament in a ceremony. In this ceremony, a couple shows a public worship. Did you ever stop to think about that? Our Christian marriages demonstrate our relationship with Christ. In this liturgical rite we recognize that marriage is to be a reflection of the relationship of Christ to His church, His bride. When we look at marriage in this manner, we may ponder what a gift we have in marriage. Marriage can be seen as a divine gift. Did you ever stop to think that God has called you to be together? In my marriage, there is not one doubt that this is the case. Perhaps, that is why I feel like my husband and I balance each other. Together with God, we become one. It may sound silly, but it's the truth. The equation always is balanced. However, it is rare that it is 50/50. There are times where it may be 0/100. During those times, God may be the one that's giving 100 percent. When we experience painful moments of loss, I can say that I was a zero and the only possible way for Chris to give 100 percent was with God's grace.

Through God's grace we are changed. Life is a different place. God chooses to enter in our lives and remains with us. This grace draws us into a closer personal relationship with Him. In serving on the pre-Cana team, we were asked to pray together as couples. I thought the priest was out of his mind. I rebelled. I just couldn't seem to do it. I would end the day with my prayers silently as I was getting ready to fall asleep. I wanted to engage in this sacred act, but I couldn't. So I prayed. We even joked about it. Clearly, through God's grace, during an anxious moment of my husband's, via text, I sent a prayer that could have been written by the Pope. He was so moved. I was so moved. He actually asked me the following day to send him another prayer while he was at work. This became a routine for about a week. I must laugh about our modern-day God who delivers grace via a Blackberry. Eventually, the text prayer became evening prayer before bed – very grace filled. Our marriage was a source for us to grow in holiness.

In my final reflection on marriage as a sacrament, I have come to see that as a married couple, my husband and I are so blessed to live out a sacrament every day. In doing so we are open to God's grace at every moment, and in living this sacrament, we take a step closer to the salvation that was brought to us from Jesus Christ. I realize that marriage is a sanctifying image, because in this sacrament, as a married couple, we conform to the Will of God. Being one is an act of holiness.

In conclusion, I think the Beatles need to add a dose of God's grace and couple it with love. If we can take our love and recognize God's grace in our marriages, we may yield an equation that yields a marriage that is indissoluble. What God has joined together, let man not separate. As you live out the sacrament of your marriage, take time to reflect on the beauty of this sacrament. Take time to embrace God's grace as He travels with you every step of the way. Always remember that God's grace, is the glue that will make each joy-filled moment the brightest that it can be, and when you are feeling less than joyous, God is with you, guiding you and redirecting you to become one – what a gift! God's grace is the gift that keeps giving. In living out the sacrament of marriage, how blessed are we?

With the close of the pre-Cana weekend, I emailed Penny and expressed thanks for her not accepting my resignation. With nothing but joy in my heart, I included this prayer:

> Heavenly Father,
>   We give thanks for calling us to serve on the pre-Cana committee.
>   We gratefully recognize that in giving we receive.
>   With humbled hearts, we ask that you continue to walk with us, as we live out our Christian marriages and that we may always be a witness to others of the sacred nature of this sacrament.
>   Help us grow in holiness as couples.
>   We ask this through Christ our Lord.
>   Amen

As I write these concluding words, I have come to realize that perhaps my "peace bubble," while it is the norm for me, may not be the norm for many. This realization truly brings me to my knees offering thanks to my ever-present companion, God. I give thanks for following His call, that led me to write day after day after day, not knowing His plan. I give thanks for having the gift of faith, which helped me realize that, yes, I am hearing the sound of God's voice, because I have silenced my heart, in order to listen. I give thanks for every moment where I had no guidance, what seemed like a lack of compassion from companions on this journey, who might have had words or not had words. I give thanks for every struggle and dark moment, because every single moment led me to growing closer to God and, in doing so, my heart is filled with great love, God's Love. It is this love that enables me to see life as a different place. A place where we are called to love all, accept all, and embrace all. This love has made me the best person God created me to be. In being my best, I am able to love myself, my husband, my children, and all I encounter with nothing but love in my heart – how beautiful.

Don't you want that beauty in your life? Just say yes to God's call. I am certain you will not regret it. The time has come. God is calling. What will you say? How will you respond?

ENDNOTES

1   Pre-Cana – A course or consultation Catholic couples must undergo before they can be married in a Catholic church.

2   Eucharistic Minister – Unordained parishioners, chosen by the parish, to assist the priest in the distribution of the elements of bread and wine at communion time during Mass.

3   Cornerstone – A spiritual retreat within the Catholic Church that encourages the development of Christ-centered relationships within our individual faith communities.

4   IEP – Individualized Education Program designed to meet the unique educational needs of one person.

5   Road to Emmaus – A road on which Jesus first appeared to two of His disciples following his Resurrection.

6   Triduum – The liturgical celebration of the three days from Holy Thursday to Easter Sunday.

7   Blessed Sacrament – A manner of honoring the true presence of Jesus in the Holy Eucharist, by exposing it with proper solemnity to the view of the faithful, in order that they may pray and be reverent before it.

8   Magnificat – A monthly pocket-sized magazine that has each day's morning and evening prayer, plus the daily readings and some other prayers.

9   Paschal Mystery – Christ's work of redemption accomplished principally by his passion, death, resurrection, and glorious ascension.

10   Novena – Nine days of prayer.

11   Pietà – A work of art that depicts Mary holding the dead body of Jesus. If you don't know Michelangelo's, get to know it. Just the sight of this work brings instant peace.